PENGUIN BOOKS

Tamarind & Saffron

Claudia Roden is the author of the highly praised *The Book of Jewish Food*, which won the André Simon Award, the Glenfiddich Food Book of the Year, the Guild of Food Writers' Food Book Award, the *Jewish Quarterly* Prize and the James Beard Award. Her other books include the seminal *A Book of Middle Eastern Food*; *Picnic*; *The Good Food of Italy – Region by Region*; *Mediterranean Cookery*; and *Coffee: A Connoisseur's Companion*. She has now won six Glenfiddich prizes for her books. She lives in London.

Tamarind & Saffron

Favourite Recipes from the Middle East

Claudia Roden

PENGUIN BOOKS

PENGUIN BOOKS

Published by the Penguin Group
Penguin Books Ltd, 80 Strand, London WC2R 0RL, England
Penguin Group (USA) Inc., 375 Hudson Street, New York, New York 10014, USA
Penguin Group (Canada), 90 Eglinton Avenue East, Suite 700, Toronto, Ontario, Canada M4P 2Y3
(a division of Pearson Penguin Canada Inc.)
Penguin Ireland, 25 St Stephen's Green, Dublin 2, Ireland (a division of Penguin Books Ltd)
Penguin Group (Australia), 250 Camberwell Road, Camberwell, Victoria 3124, Australia
(a division of Pearson Australia Group Pty Ltd)
Penguin Books India Pvt Ltd, 11 Community Centre, Panchsheel Park, New Delhi – 110 017, India
Penguin Group (NZ), 67 Apollo Drive, Rosedale, North Shore 0632, New Zealand
(a division of Pearson New Zealand Ltd)
Penguin Books (South Africa) (Pty) Ltd, 24 Sturdee Avenue, Rosebank, Johannesburg 2196, South Africa

Penguin Books Ltd, Registered Offices: 80 Strand, London WC2R 0RL, England

www.penguin.com

First published 1999
Published in Penguin Books 2000
7

Set in 11.5/14.5 Foundry Old Style
Typeset by Rowland Phototypesetting Ltd, Bury St Edmunds, Suffolk
Printed and bound in Italy by Graphicom.

ISBN: 978-0-140-46694-2

For my children and their families, Simon, Nadia and Anna, Ros and Clive, Cesar, Peter, Sarah and Ruby

Contents

Introduction

This selection of recipes represents the cooking of various countries in the Middle East. Morocco, Turkey and Lebanon, which are renowned for their cuisines, feature most prominently (each claims to have the third best after France and China). The recipes are old and traditional, but the choice of dishes is modern in that it assembles the kind of food people want to eat and cook today – delicious, exciting, wholesome and easy to prepare.

The general culture of the Middle East has it that to really please your guests you must show that you have worked very hard to prepare a meal. You have to offer an assortment of small pies, stuffed vegetables, little meatballs and the like, which require wrapping, hollowing, filling, rolling. It is almost an insult to offer something that looks as though it took little time. You can see why people have the idea that Middle Eastern food is excessively labour-intensive. But it does not have to be.

Many of the simpler dishes are really appealing. It is the special combinations of ingredients – rice and lentils with caramelized onions; bulgur (cracked wheat) with tomatoes and aubergines; artichokes and broad beans with almonds; spinach with beans or chickpeas or with yoghurt – and their delicate flavouring which make them wonderful. Although often the only flavourings are olive oil and lemon juice, every country has its traditional sets of aromatics. There is the fried garlic with cumin and coriander of Egypt; the cinnamon and allspice of Turkey; the sumac and tamarind of Syria and Lebanon; the pomegranate syrup of Iran; the preserved lemon and harissa of North Africa. The tantalizingly contradictory flavours of spicy hot with sweet of Morocco include saffron, ginger, cinnamon and cumin with hot red pepper and honey.

Another attractive side of Middle Eastern cuisines is the great use which is made of grains, vegetables, pulses, fruits, nuts and yoghurt, which are now seen as the important part of a healthy diet.

The spread of Islam in the seventh century and the establishment of an Islamic empire across Asia, North Africa, Spain and Sicily, and of the Ottoman empire over an enormous territory from the fourteenth century until the twentieth, brought a certain unity in cooking traditions and means that similar dishes appear in different countries in different regional versions.

Some of the recipes in this book are classics from *The New Book of Middle Eastern Food*. Almost half are new, and the old ones are often given in a new version. I have sometimes simplified a method. The kind of adaptation I have made is to bake pies instead of frying them; to use less butter or replace it in some dishes with oil; and to cook fish for a shorter time. I have also used an easier square shape for some large individual filo pies.

When I first came to England in the mid-fifties, no one here had eaten aubergines, let alone cooked them. I had to explain courgettes as 'baby marrows'. You could only buy products such as pitta bread, filo pastry and vine leaves in Cypriot stores in Camden Town. Certain products such as sumac, the ground red berry with a lemony flavour, tamarind paste and the sweet and sour pomegranate syrup or molasses made from the boiled-down juice of sour pomegranates were not available anywhere. Now bulgur and couscous, chickpeas and filo, are in our supermarkets as well as prepared foods such as hummus, baba ghanoush and taramasalata, falafel and filo pies, and literally every ingredient used in Middle Eastern cooking can be found in the many Middle Eastern and Indian stores which have mushroomed around our cities. And with the proliferation of Lebanese, Turkish, Persian and Moroccan restaurants, Middle Eastern food has become familiar. It has even been integrated in the menus of fashionable new restaurants offering what has come to be known as 'contemporary British' or 'modern European' food. The choice of dishes is a response to the new situation and to the reality that most people have less time to cook.

You can be flexible in the way you plan menus. Mezzes or appetizers – one of the appealing features of Middle Eastern cooking – can be served with drinks, as a first course or as side dishes. You can make a casual meal out of two or three, accompanied by bread and perhaps cheese or yoghurt and olives. A large assortment can be offered at a buffet party. The traditional drinks served with appetizers are arak (or raki), the anis-flavoured spirit distilled from grapes, and the Moroccan *mahia*, made with figs or dates. Beer too goes well with appetizers. For those who do not take alcohol, fruit juices or chilled yoghurt beaten with water or soda are traditional alternatives.

For most of the fish dishes you may use alternative kinds of fish. Feel free to use a cheaper fish or one more easily available than the one suggested. Lamb is the traditional meat of the

Middle East, but beef or veal can be used instead; and in many recipes, such as stews, meat and poultry are interchangeable. Rice, couscous and bulgur are the staples of the area. The best way to end your meal is with fresh fruit or with dried fruit and nuts. Puddings and pastries are for special occasions.

This book is all about pleasure and enjoyment but it is also a way of discovering other worlds and other cultures.

Note

Quantities are given in both imperial and metric measures. A rounded figure is generally given for the conversion – to make things easier and more comfortable – except where exactness is important to the success of a recipe or because of the weight of commercial packets, jars, tins and pots used.

Appetizers and Salads

Mezzes, as appetizers are called in Arabic, are an important feature of Middle Eastern food. Traditionally served with spirits such as the anis-flavoured arak, they are meant to provide little tastings and to sharpen the appetite, not to satisfy it. A large array can be prepared for a buffet party. They also make interesting side dishes at the dinner table.

You will find foods which can also be served as mezzes, such as filo cigars, marinated fried fish and fried fish balls, in other sections of the book.

Dukkah: An Egyptian Seed, Nut and Spice Dip

* 500g (1lb) sesame seeds
* 250g (8oz) coriander seeds
* 120g (4oz) hazelnuts
* 120g (4oz) ground cumin
* salt and pepper to taste

Dukkah (pronounced do'a*) is a dearly loved speciality in Egypt. On a recent visit to Australia I was stunned to find that it has become extremely fashionable there. Wineries produce their own blends of 'Aussie dukkah' and sell it in elegant packages. Restaurants offer it so that people can dip in with their bread soaked in olive oil. In Egypt it is served at breakfast or as an appetizer. It is a very personal and individual mix which varies from one family to another. The Aussie one is based on my mother's. It can be stored for months in covered jars.*

Put the seeds and nuts on separate trays and roast them in a preheated 250°C (500°F, gas 8) oven for 5–10 minutes or until they begin to colour and release an aroma. Put them together in the food processor with salt and pepper and grind them until they are finely crushed but not pulverized. Be careful not to over-blend or the oil from the too finely ground seeds and nuts will form a paste. Dukkah should be a crushed dry mixture, not a paste.

Variation
* Some people use peanuts or almonds instead of hazelnuts, and some add dried mint.

Bulgur and Tomato Salad

Serves 6–8

* 250g (8oz) bulgur
* 2 tablespoons tomato paste
* 5 tablespoons extra virgin olive oil
* juice of 1 lemon
* salt
* 1/3 teaspoon chilli flakes or a pinch of chilli powder to taste
* 1 fresh red or green chilli pepper, very finely chopped
* a good bunch of flat-leaf parsley, finely chopped
* a good bunch of mint, finely chopped
* 6 spring onions, finely chopped
* 2 large tomatoes, finely diced

Kisir *is the more filling and rustic Turkish equivalent of the Lebanese tabbouleh.*

In a bowl, pour plenty of boiling water on to the bulgur and leave for 30 minutes or until the grain is tender. Drain and squeeze the excess water out in a colander.

Add the tomato paste, oil and lemon juice, salt and chilli flakes or powder, and mix thoroughly. You can do this in advance.

Just before serving, mix in the rest of the ingredients.

Variation
* An added 2 tablespoons of sour pomegranate concentrate or molasses gives the grain a browny tinge and a sweet-and-sour tartness.

Tabbouleh

Serves 4

* 120g (4oz) fine bulgur
* 500g (1lb) firm ripe tomatoes, diced
* salt and pepper
* $\frac{1}{2}$ teaspoon ground cinnamon
* $\frac{1}{4}$ teaspoon ground allspice
* juice of 1 lemon or more to taste
* 4 spring onions, thinly sliced
* a large bunch of flat-leaf parsley (250g/8oz weighed with stems), finely chopped by hand
* a bunch of mint (about 70g/3oz weighed with stems), finely chopped
* 150ml (5fl oz) extra virgin olive oil
* 2 gem lettuces to garnish or for serving

This is a homely old-style version of the very green and tart parsley and mint salad you find in Lebanese restaurants. Indian and Middle Eastern stores sell large bunches of flat-leaf parsley weighing between 200 and 250g (7–9oz).

Soak the bulgur in plenty of cold water for 10 minutes. Rinse in a colander and put into a bowl with the tomatoes. Leave for 30 minutes to absorb the tomato juices. Mix gently with the rest of the ingredients except the lettuce.

A traditional way of eating tabbouleh is to scoop it up with small gem lettuce leaves or very young vine leaves.

Bread Salad

Serves 6–8

* 1½ pitta breads
* 3 medium firm ripe tomatoes, cut into 1¼cm (½in) pieces
* 3 small cucumbers, peeled, cut in half lengthways and sliced
* 1 green pepper, seeded and cut into small slices
* 5 radishes, sliced (optional)
* 1½ mild red onions or 9 spring onions, chopped
* a bunch of rocket leaves, coarsely shredded
* a bunch of purslane leaves or lamb's lettuce, coarsely shredded
* 5 cos lettuce leaves, cut into ribbons
* a small bunch of flat-leaf parsley, chopped
* a few sprigs of mint, chopped
* 5 tablespoons extra virgin olive oil
* juice of 1 lemon
* 2 garlic cloves, crushed
* salt and pepper
* 1 tablespoon ground sumac

Fattoush is a rustic country salad of Syria and Lebanon which has become part of the standard menu of Lebanese restaurants.

Cut open the pitta breads and toast them under the grill until they are crisp, turning them over once. Break them into small pieces in your hands.

Put all the vegetables into a large bowl with the rocket and purslane leaves or lamb's lettuce, cos lettuce, flat-leaf parsley and mint.

For the dressing, mix the olive oil with the lemon juice, garlic, salt, pepper and sumac.

Just before serving, add the toasted bread and toss well with the dressing.

Variation

* The old peasant way of making *fattoush* is to moisten and soften the toasted bread with water and a little lemon juice before imbuing it further with the dressing. It becomes deliciously soggy.

Rocket, Tomato and Cucumber Salad

Serves 4

* a bunch of rocket leaves, about 60g (2½oz)
* 4 plum tomatoes, quartered
* 2 small cucumbers, peeled and cut into slices or half-moons
* 1 small red onion, chopped, or 4 spring onions, sliced
* 3 tablespoons extra virgin olive oil
* 1 tablespoon wine vinegar
* salt and pepper
* 100g (4oz) feta cheese, cut into 2cm (¾in) cubes (optional)
* 8 black olives (optional)

Tear the rocket leaves and put them into a bowl with the tomatoes, cucumbers and onion. Dress with a mixture of oil, vinegar, salt and pepper.

Garnish if you like with the feta and olives.

Chopped Artichokes and Lemons

Serves 4–6

* 400g (14oz) (1 packet) frozen artichoke bottoms, defrosted
* salt
* 5 tablespoons extra virgin olive oil
* pepper
* 1–2 garlic cloves, crushed (optional)
* a few sprigs of dill, chopped
* peel of 1 preserved lemon, rinsed and chopped (see pages 84–5)

This is a splendid dish and quick to make with the frozen artichoke bottoms obtainable in Middle Eastern stores.

Boil the artichoke bottoms in salted water till tender. Drain and chop them and mix with the rest of the ingredients.
Serve cold.

Yoghurt and Cucumber Salad

Serves 6

* 4–6 small cucumbers or 1 large one, diced or cut into half-moon slices
* salt
* 500g (1lb) thick strained Greek yoghurt
* 2 garlic cloves, crushed
* 1–2 tablespoons dried crushed mint or 2 sprigs of dill, finely chopped
* white pepper

Unless the salad is to be eaten as soon as it is made, it is best to salt the cucumber and let the juices drain before mixing with the yoghurt, otherwise it gets very watery. The small cucumbers now available in supermarkets have a better flavour.

Peel and dice the cucumbers, or cut them in half lengthways, then into half-moon slices. Unless the salad is to be served immediately, sprinkle with plenty of salt and leave for 1 hour in a colander for the juices to drain.

Beat the yoghurt in a serving bowl with the garlic, mint and pepper. (Add salt later if necessary, as the cucumber is already salty.) Rinse the cucumber of excess salt if necessary, drain, then mix into the yoghurt.

Variation

* Beat 3 tablespoons of extra virgin olive oil, 1 tablespoon of vinegar and 3 tablespoons of chopped dill into the yoghurt.

Spinach and Yoghurt Salad

Serves 4

* 500g (1lb) spinach
* 225ml (8fl oz) thick strained Greek yoghurt
* 2 garlic cloves, crushed
* ¾ teaspoon sugar
* salt and pepper
* 2 tablespoons extra virgin olive oil
* juice of ½ lemon

An Iranian speciality.

Wash the spinach and remove the stems only if they are thick and hard. Drain and put in a large pan. Cover with a lid and put over a low heat until the leaves crumple into a soft mass. They steam in the water that clings to them in very few minutes.

Drain, and when cool enough, squeeze out the excess water with your hands. Chop with a sharp knife and mix with the rest of the ingredients.

Taramasalata

* 250g (9oz) smoked cod roe
* 3–4 slices of white bread, crusts removed, soaked in water
* juice of 1 lemon or to taste
* 125ml (4fl oz) mixture of ½ sunflower oil and ½ extra virgin olive oil

Grey mullet roe was once used in Turkey and Greece but smoked cod roe has generally replaced it. I like to use a mixture of sunflower and olive oil, which allows the taste of the roe to dominate.

Skin the smoked cod roe and put it through the food processor with the bread, squeezed dry, and the lemon juice.

Gradually add the oil in a thin trickle while the blades are running and blend to the consistency of mayonnaise. Cover with clingfilm and chill. If it is too liquid do not worry, it will become thick and firm after an hour or so in the refrigerator.

Hummus bi Tahina

* 180g (6oz) chickpeas, soaked in water overnight
* juice of 2 lemons, or to taste
* 2–3 garlic cloves, crushed
* salt
* 4 tablespoons tahina (sesame paste)

This chickpea purée (hummus) with sesame paste (tahina) is the most popular and widely known Middle Eastern dip.

Drain the soaked chickpeas and boil in fresh water for about 1 hour, or until they are soft. Drain, reserving the cooking water. Blend the chickpeas to a purée in the food processor. Add the remaining ingredients and a little of the cooking water – enough to blend to a soft creamy paste. Taste and adjust the seasoning. Add more lemon juice, garlic or salt if necessary.

Pour the cream into a flat dish and serve with Arab bread or pitta.

Optional garnishes
* Dribble 2 tablespoons of extra virgin olive oil over, and sprinkle on 1 teaspoon of paprika or 1 tablespoon of finely chopped flat-leaf parsley.
* Garnish with a pinch of hot chilli powder and 1/2 teaspoon of ground cumin, making a star design of alternating red and brown.
* Sprinkle with a few whole cooked chickpeas, put aside before blending.
* Sprinkle with ground sumac and a little chopped flat-leaf parsley.
* This is a delicious hot version. Pour the hummus bi tahina into a shallow baking dish. Fry 2 tablespoons of pine nuts lightly in 2 tablespoons of butter and sprinkle them with the melted butter over the dish. Bake for about 20 minutes in a 200°C (400°F, gas 6) oven.

Falafel

Serves 10

* 500g (1lb 2oz) dried split broad beans, soaked in cold water for 24 hours
* salt and pepper
* 2 teaspoons ground cumin
* 1 teaspoon ground coriander
* a pinch of chilli powder (optional)
* 1 teaspoon bicarbonate of soda
* 1 large onion, very finely chopped or grated
* 5 spring onions, very finely chopped
* 6 cloves garlic, crushed
* a large bunch of flat-leaf parsley, finely chopped
* a large bunch of coriander, finely chopped
* sunflower or light vegetable oil for deep-frying

These flavoursome broad bean rissoles, called ta'amia *in Cairo, are a national dish of Egypt. You must buy the large broad beans which are sold already skinned as 'split broad beans' in Middle Eastern stores.*

The long soaking of the beans to soften them is all-important. Drain the beans very well and let them dry out a little on a towel. Then put them through the food processor until they form a paste, adding salt and pepper, cumin, coriander, chilli powder and bicarbonate of soda. The paste must be so smooth and soft that it will hold together when you fry it. Let it rest for at least 30 minutes.

Add the rest of the ingredients except the oil. If you chop or grate the onions in the food processor, strain them to get rid of the juice.

Knead the mixture well with your hands. Take small lumps and make flat, round shapes 5cm (2in) in diameter and $^1/_2$cm ($^1/_4$in) thick. Let them rest for 15 minutes, then fry them in deep hot oil until they are crisp and brown, turning them over once. Lift out with a slotted spoon and drain on kitchen paper.

Serve hot, accompanied by hummus (page 11) or baba ghanoush (page 13), a tomato and cucumber salad and pitta bread.

Note

If the paste does not hold together it usually means that it has not been properly mashed. You can remedy this by adding 2–3 tablespoons of flour.

Baba Ghanoush

Serves 4–6
* 1kg (2lb) aubergines
* 2–3 garlic cloves, crushed (optional)
* salt
* 4 tablespoons tahina (sesame paste)
* juice of 2 lemons, or more to taste

This dip, also called moutabal, *is offered as a mezze in every Arab restaurant.*

Grill or roast the aubergines until very soft inside (see below). Peel them in a colander, then chop the flesh with a pointed knife and mash it with a fork, letting the bitter juices run out through the holes in the colander.

Add the garlic, a little salt, the tahina and lemon juice, beating well and tasting to adjust the flavouring. You may use a food processor.

Pour the cream into a shallow dish and serve with Arab or pitta bread to dip in.

Optional garnish
* 1 tablespoon of finely chopped flat-leaf parsley and a dribble of 2 tablespoons extra virgin olive oil.

To roast and mash whole aubergines

Prick the aubergines in a few places with a pointed knife so that they do not burst. Turn them under the grill for about 20 minutes until the skin is black and blistered and they feel very soft inside when you press them, or roast them in the hottest possible oven for about 30 minutes or until they feel very soft, turning them at least once. When cool enough to handle, peel them in a colander. Then chop the flesh with a knife and mash it with a fork in the colander to let the juices escape.

Aubergine Purée with Olive Oil and Lemon

Serves 4

* 2 aubergines (about 500g/1lb)
* 2 tablespoons extra virgin olive oil
* juice of ½ lemon or to taste
* salt

This is one of the simplest, most common and most delicious ways of eating aubergines. Use firm aubergines with a shiny black skin. In the variations, pomegranate molasses, which are also called concentrate or syrup in Middle Eastern stores, are the boiled-down concentrated juice of sour pomegranates.

Grill or roast the aubergines (see page 13). Peel them in a colander, then chop and mash the flesh to a purée with a fork or a wooden spoon, letting the juices escape through the holes of the colander.

Beat in the oil and lemon juice and some salt.

Serve cold.

Variations

* For a Turkish version add 2 crushed garlic cloves and 3 tablespoons of thick strained Greek yoghurt. Reduce the olive oil to 1 tablespoon.
* For a spicy Moroccan version add 1 crushed garlic clove, ½ teaspoon of harissa (see page 171, or a pinch of cayenne and ½ teaspoon of paprika), ½ teaspoon of ground cumin and a tablespoon of chopped coriander leaves.
* For a Syrian flavour mix in 2 tablespoons of pomegranate molasses instead of lemon juice.
* Add 3 tablespoons of flat-leaf parsley, 1 chopped tomato, 4 chopped spring onions and ½–1 finely chopped (and seeded) fresh chilli pepper.

Grilled Aubergine Slices with Yoghurt

Serves 4

* 3 medium aubergines (about 750g/1½lb)
* mild extra virgin olive oil or a light vegetable oil
* salt
* 400ml (14fl oz) thick strained Greek yoghurt

In Turkey the aubergines are always deep-fried, but they are also good grilled as long as they are not undercooked, and they don't need salting (see page 16). I prefer the yoghurt plain but you may like a touch of garlic and mint.

Peel the aubergines (the peel remains tough when it is grilled) and cut them lengthways into slices about 1cm (⅓in) thick. Brush generously with oil, or pour some oil on a plate and turn each slice in it so that they absorb as much as they need.

Sprinkle with salt and arrange on a tray under a preheated grill. Cook for about 15 minutes, turning over once. Or cook on an oiled griddle pan. Make sure the slices are really tender.

Serve hot or cold, with yoghurt spread thickly over.

Variation
* Beat into the yoghurt 1 crushed garlic clove and 2 teaspoons of dried crushed mint.

Grilled Aubergine Slices with Tomato Sauce

Serves 4

* 3 medium aubergines (about 750g/1½lb)
* mild extra virgin olive oil or a light vegetable oil
* salt
* 4 garlic cloves, crushed
* 750g (1½lb) tomatoes, peeled and chopped
* 2 tablespoons red or white wine vinegar
* 1 tablespoon sugar
* a good pinch of chilli powder
* a bunch of flat-leaf parsley, chopped

Although fried aubergines have a better taste, grilled ones, which are lighter and less oily, will do very well in this recipe. About salting aubergines, see below.

Peel the aubergines (the peel remains tough when it is grilled) and cut them lengthways into slices about 1cm (⅓in) thick. Brush generously with oil, or pour some oil on to a plate and turn the slices in it so that they absorb as much as they need. Sprinkle with salt and arrange on a tray under a preheated grill. Cook for 15 minutes, turning over at least once. Or cook on an oiled griddle pan. Make sure the slices are really tender.

For the sauce, fry the garlic in 2 tablespoons of oil for a few seconds, stirring. Add the tomatoes, vinegar, sugar, salt and chilli powder, and cook, uncovered, over a low heat for about 20–30 minutes or until reduced to a thick sauce. Add the parsley and leave to cool.

Serve the aubergine slices cold, covered with the tomato sauce.

Salting aubergines

In the Middle East and in most countries where aubergines are common, the custom is to salt the aubergines to rid them of their bitter juices and also to make them absorb less oil. There are two traditional ways. One is to soak them in salted water for ½–1 hour; another is to sprinkle them with plenty of salt, leave them in a colander to degorge their juices, then rinse and dry them.

Lately, I have experimented with batches of aubergines to ➤

Grilled Aubergine Slices with Pomegranate Dressing

Serves 4

* 3 medium aubergines (about 750g/1½lb)
* mild extra virgin olive oil or a light vegetable oil
* salt
* 2 tablespoons sour pomegranate concentrate or molasses
* 1–2 garlic cloves, crushed

These have a Syrian flavour.

Peel the aubergines (the peel remains tough when it is grilled) and cut them lengthways into slices about 1cm (¹/₃in) thick. Brush generously with oil, or pour some oil on to a plate and turn the slices in it so that they absorb as much as they need. Sprinkle lightly with salt and arrange on a tray under a preheated grill. Cook for 15 minutes, turning over at least once. Or cook on an oiled griddle pan. Make sure the slices are really tender.

Mix the sour pomegranate concentrate with the garlic and about 2 tablespoons of water, and pour a little over each slice, arranged flat on a dish.

Serve cold.

---

see if salting really makes a difference and found that, with the aubergines I used, it did not. You can get the occasional rare very bitter aubergine (the way they are grown today makes it very unlikely), and in that case it would make a difference. Aubergines – even if they have been salted – absorb a lot of oil when they are fried.

Nowadays I prefer to grill or roast aubergines or to fry them only very briefly in very hot oil before stewing them, in which case salting is not really necessary.

Aubergines in a Spicy Honey Sauce

Serves 4

* 2 medium to large aubergines
* olive oil
* salt
* 3 garlic cloves, crushed
* 5cm (2in) fresh root ginger, grated or crushed in a garlic press to extract the juice
* 1½ teaspoons ground cumin
* a large pinch of cayenne or chilli powder, to taste
* 6 tablespoons liquid honey
* juice of 1 lemon
* 150ml (¼ pint) water

The sauce is a delicious example of the hot, spicy and sweet combinations which are a thrilling feature of North African cooking.

Peel the aubergines (the peel remains tough when it is grilled) and cut them into rounds about 1cm (⅓in) thick. Dip them in olive oil, turning them over, and sprinkle with salt. Cook on a griddle pan or under the grill, turning them over once, until they are lightly browned. They do not need to be very soft, as they will cook further in the sauce.

In a wide saucepan or frying pan, fry the garlic in 2 tablespoons of the oil for seconds only, stirring, then take off the heat. Add the ginger, cumin, cayenne or chilli powder, honey, lemon juice and water. Put in the aubergine slices and cook over a low heat, either in batches so that they are in one layer, or together – rearranging them so that each slice gets some time in the sauce – for about 10 minutes or until the slices are soft and have absorbed the sauce. Add a little more water if necessary.

Serve cold with bread.

Right Roasted red peppers with preserved lemon and capers
Overleaf Broad beans with rice and yoghurt

Spicy Aubergine Salad

Serves 6

* 750g (1½lb) aubergines, peeled and cubed
* 5 garlic cloves, peeled
* salt
* 3 large beef tomatoes (about 750g/1½lb), peeled and chopped
* 4 tablespoons argan oil or extra virgin olive oil
* 2 tablespoons wine vinegar
* ½ teaspoon harissa (see page 171) or a mixture of ½ teaspoon paprika and a good pinch of cayenne, or to taste
* 1 teaspoon ground cumin
* a bunch of flat-leaf parsley, chopped

This Moroccan salad called zaalouk *(*ajlouk *in Tunisia) is best made several hours in advance so that the flavours have time to really penetrate. The aubergines are boiled, so the salad is not oily. In Morocco they may use argan oil, a very rare oil with a delicate nutty flavour, made from the nut inside the fruit of the argan tree which grows only in the Souss (south-west) region of Morocco. I was offered a sample recently by the Fresh Olive Company and I hope it will be available in this country through them.*

Boil the aubergines with the garlic in plenty of salted water, in a pan with a lid, for about 30 minutes or until they are very soft. Drain and chop the aubergines and garlic in a colander then mash them with a fork, pressing all the water out.

Put the chopped tomatoes into the emptied pan and cook on a low heat for about 20 minutes or until reduced to a thick sauce, stirring occasionally. Mix with the mashed aubergines and the rest of the ingredients, and add salt.

Variation
* Add the juice of 1 lemon (instead of the vinegar), and 1 teaspoon of ground caraway or ground coriander.

Previous page **Egg and lemon fish soup** Left Grilled aubergine slices with tomato sauce and with yoghurt; aubergine purée with olive oil and lemon

Roast Pepper and Tomato Salad

Serves 6

* 3 red or green peppers
* 5 garlic cloves, whole and unpeeled
* 3 large tomatoes, peeled and diced
* a bunch of coriander leaves, chopped
* 4 tablespoons argan oil (see page 19) or extra virgin olive oil
* 1 tablespoon vinegar or juice of ½ lemon
* salt and pepper
* ½–1 teaspoon ground cumin

Every country in the Middle East has a roast pepper and tomato combination. This is a North African version.

Roast the peppers under the grill and peel them (see page 21). At the same time grill the garlic cloves until they just begin to feel soft, turning them over once.

Cut the peppers into tiny squares and chop the garlic. Put into a serving bowl with the tomatoes and chopped coriander.

Just before serving, dress with a mixture of oil and vinegar or lemon juice, salt, pepper and cumin.

Variation
* Add 2 tablespoons of capers and half the peel of a preserved lemon (page 84), cut into small pieces.

Roasted Red Peppers with Preserved Lemon and Capers

Serves 4

* 4 fleshy red peppers
* 2–3 tablespoons argan oil (see page 19) or extra virgin olive oil
* salt
* peel of 1 preserved lemon, cut into small pieces (see page 84)
* 2 tablespoons capers

These peppers are wonderful.

Roast, seed and peel the peppers as described below, and cut them into strips about 1½cm (²⁄₃in) wide. Dress with the oil and a very little salt, and garnish with the preserved lemon and capers.

Variation

* For roasted peppers with pomegranate dressing, dress with a mixture of 1 tablespoon of pomegranate molasses and 2 tablespoons of extra virgin olive oil and sprinkle with a very little salt.

To roast and peel peppers

Many dishes call for roasted red peppers (red ones are riper and have a better taste). Choose fleshy peppers. Put them on an oven tray under the grill, about 9cm (3½in) from the heat (or grill them on the barbecue). Turn them until their skins are black and blistered all over.

Alternatively, it is easier to roast them in the hottest possible oven for about 30 minutes or until they are soft and their skins begin to blister and blacken – they need to be turned once on their side. To loosen the skins further, put them in a strong polythene bag, twist it closed and leave for 10–15 minutes. Another old way which has the same effect is to put them in a pan with a tight-fitting lid.

When the peppers are cool enough to handle, peel them and remove the stems and seeds. Keep the juice that comes out and strain to remove the seeds, as it can be used as part of the dressing.

Roast peppers can be kept for a long time in a jar, covered in oil.

Tunisian Roasted Salad

Serves 4–6

* 3 medium onions
* 3 green or red bell peppers
* 3 medium tomatoes (about 250g/8oz), peeled and quartered
* 1 × 200g (7oz) tin of tuna in brine, drained
* 2 hard-boiled eggs, cut in wedges
* 4–5 tablespoons extra virgin olive oil
* juice of 1 lemon
* salt and pepper
* ½ teaspoon caraway seeds
* 1 tablespoon capers
* 8 green or black olives

They call this meshweya (roasted) because the vegetables are roasted – usually over a fire. There are many versions. This one is a substantial meal in itself.

Put the onions and peppers in the hottest preheated oven and roast for about 30 minutes or until the skins are very brown and they feel soft, turning them over on their sides. Or turn them under the grill. Peel the onions and cut them in wedges. Peel the peppers (see page 21) and cut them into ribbons.

On a serving dish or individual plates arrange the elements of the salad – the onions, peppers, tomatoes, flaked tuna and eggs – in a decorative way. Mix the oil and lemon, salt, pepper and caraway seeds and dribble on top.

Garnish with capers and olives.

Mashed Courgettes and Tomatoes

Serves 6

* 2 large onions, chopped
* 4 tablespoons extra virgin olive oil
* 2 garlic cloves, crushed
* 1 teaspoon ground cumin
* 500g (1lb) courgettes, cut into thick slices
* salt and pepper
* 2 tablespoons red or white wine vinegar
* a good pinch of chilli powder
* 500g (1lb) tomatoes, peeled and chopped

A North African appetizer.

Fry the onion in the oil until golden and stir in the garlic and cumin. Add the courgettes, salt, pepper, vinegar, chilli powder and tomatoes. Put the lid on and cook for about 10 minutes without added water, until the courgettes are very soft.

Mash with a fork or a potato masher and serve at room temperature.

Courgettes with Onions, Garlic and Mint

Serves 6–8

* 1kg (2lb) courgettes, cut into large pieces
* about 750ml (1¼ pints) chicken stock (use 2 stock cubes)
* 2 onions, chopped
* 3 tablespoons extra virgin olive oil
* 4 garlic cloves, crushed
* 2 tablespoons chopped mint leaves
* salt and pepper
* 1 lemon, cut in wedges (optional)

This is good hot or cold, as an appetizer served with bread, or as a side dish.

Boil the courgettes in the stock for about 15 minutes or until soft. Drain, mash and chop the courgettes in a colander to get rid of the excess liquid (I drink it – it has a lovely courgette flavour).

In a large frying pan, fry the onions in 2 tablespoons of the oil until golden. Add the garlic and stir until it just begins to colour. Add the courgettes, mint, salt and pepper and cook, stirring and mixing well for about 5 minutes.

Stir in the remaining oil and serve hot or cold with lemon wedges.

Variation

* Stir in 500ml (18fl oz) thick strained Greek yoghurt before serving, or pass the pot round for everyone to help themselves.

Baby Onions in Tamarind

Serves 6

* 500g (1lb) shallots or pickling
  onions
* 2 tablespoons olive oil
* 1 tablespoon tamarind paste
* 1 tablespoon sugar

You can find tamarind paste in Middle Eastern and Indian stores. It gives the onions an intense sweet-and-sour taste.

Poach the onions in boiling water for about 5 minutes (this makes them easier to peel) and peel them when just cool enough to handle.

In a pan just large enough to contain them in one layer, sauté the onions in the oil, shaking the pan and turning them to brown them lightly all over.

Add the tamarind and the sugar and half cover with water. Stir well and cook, covered, over a low heat for about 25 minutes or until very soft, adding water if necessary, and lifting the lid and reducing the sauce over a high heat at the end.

Serve cold.

Walnut and Pomegranate Paste

Serves 6–8

* 150g (5oz) shelled walnuts
* 1½–2 tablespoons tomato paste
* 1 slice of wholemeal bread, crusts removed and lightly toasted
* 120ml (4fl oz) extra virgin olive oil
* 2 tablespoons pomegranate syrup
* 1 teaspoon coarsely ground red pepper flakes or a pinch of chilli powder
* 1 teaspoon ground cumin
* 2 teaspoons sugar
* salt

There are many versions of this exquisite Turkish relish called muhammara, *which can also be found in Syria and Lebanon. It can be served with bread as an appetizer or to accompany grilled meat or fish or cold vegetables. Make sure that the walnuts taste fresh.*

Blend the walnuts with all the other ingredients in the food processor.

Spicy Carrot Purée

Serves 6

* 750g (1½lb) carrots
* salt
* 4 tablespoons extra virgin olive oil
* 3 tablespoons wine vinegar
* 2 garlic cloves, crushed
* 1 teaspoon harissa (see page 171), or 1 teaspoon paprika and a good pinch of chilli powder, or to taste
* 1½ teaspoons ground cumin or caraway seeds

A peppery Tunisian salad called omi houriya.

Peel the carrots and cut into large pieces. Boil them in salted water until tender, then drain and mash them with a fork or chop them, and add the rest of the ingredients.

Serve cold.

Optional garnishes
* 6 black olives.
* 100g (4oz) feta cheese, cut into small cubes.

Celeriac and Carrots with a Hazelnut and Yoghurt Sauce

Serves 4–6

* 1 large celeriac
* 3 large carrots
* salt

For the sauce

* 100g (4oz) hazelnuts, coarsely ground
* 2 garlic cloves, crushed
* 4 tablespoons extra virgin olive oil
* 3 tablespoons white wine vinegar
* 150ml (¼ pint) thick strained Greek yoghurt

This beautiful fresh-tasting salad is Turkish. The sauce is one of several with nuts called tarator.

Peel the celeriac and carrots and cut into matchsticks. Boil in salted water for a short time until just tender and drain.

For the sauce, mix the nuts with the rest of the ingredients. Serve the vegetables with the sauce poured over.

Celeriac with Turmeric

Serves 4–6

* 2 celeriac (about 1kg/2lb)
* 3 garlic cloves, crushed
* 5 tablespoons extra virgin olive oil
* ¼ teaspoon turmeric
* salt and pepper
* 2 teaspoons sugar
* juice of 1 lemon

The celeriac has a delicate sweet-and-sour flavour and a pale yellow tinge.

Peel and wash the celeriac and cut into pieces of roughly the same size. Put them into a saucepan with the rest of the ingredients and enough water to cover.

Cook, uncovered, for 10–15 minutes over a low heat until the celeriac is soft and the liquid is absorbed, turning the pieces over and raising the heat, if necessary, to reduce the sauce a little at the end.

Serve cold.

Stuffed Vine Leaves

Makes 30–35

* 250g (8oz) preserved, drained vine leaves
* 250g (8oz) long-grain rice
* 2–3 tomatoes, skinned and chopped
* 1 large onion, finely chopped, or 4 tablespoons finely chopped spring onions
* 2 tablespoons finely chopped flat-leaf parsley
* 2 tablespoons dried crushed mint
* 1/4 level teaspoon ground cinnamon
* 1/4 level teaspoon ground allspice
* salt and pepper
* 2 tomatoes, sliced (optional)
* 3–4 cloves garlic (optional)
* 150ml (1/4 pint) olive oil
* 1/4 teaspoon powdered saffron or turmeric (optional)
* 1 teaspoon sugar
* juice of 1 lemon, or more, to taste

This is my mother's recipe from Egypt. It is especially aromatic.

If using vine leaves preserved in brine, put them in a bowl and pour boiling water over them. Leave them to soak for 15 minutes, then change the water twice, using fresh cold water. If using fresh leaves, plunge a few at a time into boiling water for a few seconds until they become limp, then lift them out.

Pour boiling water over the rice and stir well, then rinse under the cold tap and drain. Mix the rice with the tomatoes, onion or spring onions, parsley, mint, cinnamon, allspice and salt and pepper to taste.

Stuff the leaves with this mixture. Place each leaf on a plate vein side up. Put one heaped teaspoonful of filling in the centre of the leaf near the stem end. Fold the stem end up over the filling, then fold both sides towards the middle and roll up like a small cigar. Squeeze lightly in the palm of your hand. Fill the rest of the leaves in the same way.

Pack them tightly into a large pan lined with tomato slices or leftover, torn or imperfect vine leaves, occasionally slipping a whole clove of garlic in between them if you like.

Mix the olive oil with 150ml (1/4 pint) of water and the saffron or turmeric, if using. Add the sugar and lemon juice, and pour the mixture over the stuffed leaves. Put a small plate on top of the leaves to prevent them unwinding, cover the pan, and simmer very gently for about 1 hour, until the rolls are thoroughly cooked, adding water occasionally, a coffee-cup at a time, as the liquid in the pan becomes absorbed. Cool in the pan before turning out. Serve cold.

Variation

* Raisins or currants and pine nuts – about 60g (2oz) of each – may be added to the filling.

Brown Lentils and Rice with Caramelized Onions

Serves 4–6

* 3 large onions (about 750g/1½lb), cut in half and sliced
* 125ml (4fl oz) olive oil
* 250g (8oz) large brown lentils
* 250g (8oz) long-grain rice
* salt and pepper

Megadarra *is very popular in Egypt (in Syria and Lebanon it is pronounced* mujaddara*). Serve it as a starter, accompanied by yoghurt. The large quantity of dark caramelized onions makes it especially wonderful.*

Fry the onions in 3–4 tablespoons of the oil, stirring often, until they turn a rich golden brown.

Rinse the lentils and cook in 1 litre (1³/4 pints) of water for 20 minutes. Now add half the fried onions and the rice. Season with salt and pepper and stir well. Put the lid on and cook on a very low heat for another 20 minutes or until the rice and lentils are tender, adding water if they become too dry.

At the same time put the remaining onions back on the heat and continue to fry them, stirring often, until they are a dark brown and almost caramelized.

Serve with the remaining oil stirred into the rice and lentils and the fried onions sprinkled on top.

Variations

* Add 1 tablespoon of tomato paste and ¹/2 teaspoon of dried red pepper flakes or ¹/4 teaspoon of chilli powder to the water with the lentils.
* For **Lentils with Bulgur** use bulgur instead of rice.

Broad Beans with Rice and Yoghurt

Serves 4

* 250g (8oz) American long-grain rice
* salt
* 4–5 tablespoons sunflower or mild extra virgin olive oil
* a bunch of dill or mint, finely chopped
* white pepper
* 400g (14oz) shelled broad beans
* 400ml (14fl oz) yoghurt
* 1 garlic clove, crushed (optional)

An Iranian grocer near where I live sells frozen shelled and skinned broad beans from Iran. I buy them when I can't find young fresh ones. They have a wonderful flavour and texture. Do look for them. The dish can be served hot or cold. If it is to be served hot, use sunflower oil, if cold use olive oil. The yoghurt can be served poured over the rice or in a separate bowl.

Pour the rice into boiling salted water. Boil hard for about 14 minutes until it is almost but not entirely tender. Drain and put back into the pan. Stir in 3 tablespoons of the oil, the herbs, and salt and pepper to taste. Put the lid on and leave the pan on a very low heat for the rice to steam for about 15 minutes or until tender.

Boil the broad beans in salted water for a few minutes until tender, then drain. Stir gently into the rice with the remaining oil.

Serve hot or cold with the yoghurt – beaten with crushed garlic and a little salt – poured over.

Rice Salad with Tomatoes and Aubergines

Serves 6

* 1 large onion, chopped
* 5 tablespoons extra virgin olive oil
* 5 tomatoes (about 400g/14oz), peeled and chopped
* 1 teaspoon sugar
* ½ teaspoon ground allspice
* a pinch of chilli flakes or powder (optional)
* salt
* 250g (8oz) rice
* 2 aubergines (about 500g/1lb), cut into 2½cm (1in) cubes
* sunflower oil to fry the aubergines
* a sprig of dill, chopped
* a sprig of mint, chopped

In a large pan fry the onion in 2 tablespoons of the olive oil till soft. Add the tomatoes, sugar, allspice and chilli, and cook over a low heat for 10 minutes.

Add 340ml (12fl oz) of water, stir in some salt and bring to the boil. Add the rice, stir, and cook, covered, over a low heat for about 20 minutes, until the rice is tender and the liquid absorbed, adding a little water if it becomes too dry and begins to stick.

In the meantime, deep-fry the aubergines in oil to cover, turning them over once, until lightly browned. Drain on kitchen paper.

When the rice is done, stir in the dill and mint, the remaining extra virgin olive oil and the aubergines. Put the lid on and cook for a few minutes more. Serve cold.

Soups

Soups are sold by street vendors for breakfast in the early morning. They are also served at weddings and celebrations.

Green Vegetable Soup with Garlic, Mint and Lemon

Serves 6–8

* 2 litres (3½ pints) chicken stock (you may use 2 stock cubes)
* 3 leeks, cut into 2cm (¾in) slices
* 1 head of celery with leaves, cut into 2cm (¾in) slices
* 4 potatoes, peeled and diced
* salt and white pepper
* 4 garlic cloves, chopped
* juice of 1–3 lemons, to taste
* 1 teaspoon sugar, or more to taste
* 4 courgettes, cut in 1cm (½in) slices
* 2 tablespoons dried mint

This tangy aromatic soup is Egyptian.

Bring the stock to the boil in a pan. Put in the leeks, celery, and potatoes. Add salt, pepper, the garlic, lemon juice and sugar and simmer for about 30 minutes.

Add the courgettes and mint and cook for 15 minutes more.

Yoghurt Soup with Rice and Chickpeas

Serves 6

* 100g (4oz) rice
* salt
* 1.2 litres (2 pints) chicken stock (you may use 2 stock cubes)
* 450ml (15 fl oz) thick strained Greek yoghurt
* 2 tablespoons flour
* 2 egg yolks
* pepper
* 400g (14oz) tin of chickpeas, drained

In this Turkish soup, the egg yolk and flour prevent the yoghurt from curdling. The rice is best cooked separately and added at the end, as it gets bloated and mushy if left in the soup too long.

Cook the rice in boiling salted water until tender and drain.

Bring the chicken stock to the boil in a large pan.

In a bowl beat the yoghurt with the flour and egg yolks until blended and add salt and pepper. Pour this into the stock, stirring vigorously. Continue to stir, over a very low heat, until the soup thickens slightly.

Before serving, add the rice and chickpeas and heat through.

Variations

* Heat 2 tablespoons of butter or olive oil, stir in 2 tablespoons of paprika, and dribble a little over each serving.
* Add a pinch of saffron pistils or $1/4$ teaspoon of turmeric and 1–2 crushed garlic cloves to the stock and simmer for a few minutes.
* An Iranian version adds $1/4$ teaspoon of turmeric and a variety of chopped herbs, including flat-leaf parsley, tarragon and chives, as well as shredded spinach.

Tomato and Rice Soup with Mint and Coriander

Serves 4

* 75g (3oz) rice
* salt
* 1 onion, chopped
* 2 tablespoons olive oil
* 2 garlic cloves
* 1 teaspoon tomato paste
* 1kg (2¼lb) tomatoes
* 1 teaspoon sugar
* ½ litre chicken stock (you may use a stock cube)
* a bunch of coriander, finely chopped
* a few sprigs of mint, finely chopped

An Egyptian soup. It is best to cook the rice separately and add it just before serving, as it gets too bloated and soft if it stands in the soup.

Pour the rice into boiling salted water and cook for 18 minutes or until tender, then drain.

In a large pan, fry the onion in the oil until soft. Add the garlic and stir until the aroma rises, then stir in the tomato paste and take off the heat.

Cut the tomatoes in quarters and, without peeling them, blend them to a cream in the food processor. Pour them into the pan.

Add sugar and the stock and cook for about 20 minutes.

Just before serving add the cooked rice, chopped coriander and mint.

Egg and Lemon Fish Soup

Serves 6

* 1½ litres (2½ pints) stock (use 2 fish or chicken stock cubes)
* ¼ teaspoon powdered saffron or saffron pistils (optional)
* 50g (2oz) vermicelli, broken into small pieces, or little pasta grains (they are called birds' tongues in Arabic because that is what they look like)
* 900g (2lb) skinned fish fillets or a mixture with cooked prawns and mussels
* 3 eggs
* juice of 1–2 lemons
* salt and pepper

You find this in many Middle Eastern countries. In Greece it is the famous avgolemono. *Use skinned fish fillets – white fish such as cod or haddock – or a mixture of seafood including cooked peeled prawns and, if you like, a handful of shelled mussels. (You can buy cleaned and cooked mussels in many supermarkets.)*

Bring the stock to the boil in a large pan. Add the saffron, vermicelli and fish fillets (not the cooked seafood) and cook for 5–10 minutes until the vermicelli is tender and the fish begins to flake. Now add the seafood, if using, and bring to the boil, then take off the heat.

In a bowl, beat the eggs with the lemon juice. Add a ladleful of the liquid soup and beat well. Pour the egg mixture into the soup and stir for a minute or so over a low heat, until the soup thickens a little. Do not let it boil or the eggs will curdle. Taste and add salt and pepper.

Serve at once.

Variation

* A Tunisian version has 1 tablespoon of tomato paste, 2 large boiled potatoes cut into pieces, and 3 tablespoons of chopped flat-leaf parsley or coriander added to the stock.

Spicy Lentil Soup

This is an Egyptian favourite.

Serves 6–8

* 1 large onion, chopped
* 3 tablespoons olive oil
* 3 garlic cloves, crushed
* 1–1½ teaspoons ground cumin
* 1 teaspoon ground coriander
* a pinch of chilli powder
* 375g (13oz) split red lentils
* a bunch of celery leaves,
  chopped
* 1 carrot, finely chopped
* 2 litres (3½ pints) chicken stock
  (you may use 2 stock cubes)
* salt and pepper
* juice of ½–1 lemon

To garnish

* 1½ large onions, sliced
* 2–3 tablespoons olive oil
* 1 toasted pitta bread, broken
  into small pieces, to serve as
  croûtons (optional)
* 2 lemons, cut into wedges

Soften the onion in the oil in a large saucepan. Add the garlic, cumin, coriander and chilli powder and stir.

Add the lentils, celery leaves and carrot, cover with the stock, and simmer for 30–45 minutes, until the lentils have disintegrated. Taste, season with salt and pepper and add water if the soup needs thinning (it should be quite thin). Stir in the lemon juice.

For the garnish, fry the onions in the oil over a medium heat, stirring occasionally, until crisp and very brown – almost caramelized. Garnish each serving with a heaped tablespoon of the onions and serve with lemon wedges and croûtons for people to help themselves.

Lemony Spinach and Lentil Soup

Serves 6

* 1 large onion, chopped
* 2 tablespoons olive oil
* 3 garlic cloves, finely chopped
* 250g (9oz) large brown lentils
* 2 medium potatoes, diced
* 2 litres (3½ pints) water or stock (you may use 2 vegetable or chicken stock cubes)
* 500g (1lb) spinach or chard leaves
* a large bunch of coriander, chopped
* salt and pepper
* juice of 1½ lemons or more to taste

This is the popular Lebanese soup shorbet adass bi hamud.

In a large pan, fry the onion in the oil until soft and golden. Add the garlic and stir until it begins to colour. Add the lentils and potatoes, and the water or stock, and simmer for 25 minutes or until the lentils are tender.

Wash the spinach or chard leaves and shred. An easy way to cut spinach is to put it into a pan with the lid on, and only the water that clings to the leaves, over a low heat, until the leaves collapse into a soft mass which is easy to chop. Add the spinach or chard to the pan with the coriander. Add water if necessary, and season with salt and pepper.

Cook for a few minutes more and add lemon juice to taste before serving.

Variation

* For *adass bi rishta* (with noodles), add 75g (3oz) tagliatelle broken into 2½cm (1in) pieces when the lentils have begun to soften.

Moroccan Chicken and Chickpea Soup

Serves 8–10

* 1 chicken
* 250g (8oz) chickpeas, soaked in water for at least 1 hour or overnight
* 1 large onion, coarsely chopped
* 300g (11oz) tomatoes, peeled and chopped
* pepper
* $^1/_2$–$^3/_4$ teaspoon ground ginger
* 1 teaspoon ground cinnamon
* 200g (7oz) large green lentils, rinsed
* salt
* 100g (4oz) vermicelli, crushed into bits with your hand
* a large bunch of flat-leaf parsley, coarsely chopped
* a large bunch of coriander, coarsely chopped
* 2 lemons, cut in wedges, to serve

This Moroccan harira *makes a lovely and nutritious evening meal.*

Put the chicken and the chickpeas into a large pan with 3 litres (5$^1/_2$ pints) of water. Bring to the boil and remove the scum, then add the onion, tomatoes and some pepper and simmer, covered, for 1 hour or until the chickpeas are tender.

Lift out the chicken, remove the skin and bones, and cut up the meat into pieces.

Add the ginger, cinnamon and lentils, and cook for 20 minutes or until the lentils are tender, adding salt when they are.

Return the chicken to the pan and add more water. Add the vermicelli and cook for a few minutes until they are just tender.

Just before serving, add the parsley and coriander. Serve with lemon wedges.

Note

Here are two traditional ways of thickening the soup if you wish to do so.

* Beat 3 eggs vigorously with a little of the broth from the soup and pour this into the pan, stirring vigorously for a few seconds without letting the soup boil (or the eggs will curdle).
* Add 4 tablespoons of flour mixed to a light cream with a few tablespoons of cold water, and stir vigorously for 5 minutes.

Moroccan Pumpkin Soup

Serves 6

* 1¼kg (2½lb) piece of orange pumpkin
* 750ml (1¼ pints) chicken stock (you may use 2 stock cubes)
* 750ml (1¼ pints) milk
* salt and white pepper
* 2–3 teaspoons sugar, or to taste
* 120g (1oz) cooked rice, weighed uncooked (optional)
* 1 teaspoon cinnamon to garnish

This delicate and beautiful soup is made with the large orange pumpkin, which is sold cut up into large slices. Ask to taste a bit from an open one, as the taste varies. You will know if it is not very good.

Remove the peel, seeds and fibre from the pumpkin and cut it into pieces. Put it in a large pan with the stock and the milk, season with salt, pepper and sugar and simmer for 15–20 minutes until it is tender. Lift the pumpkin out, purée in a food processor, and return to the pan.

Bring to the boil again, throw in the rice and simmer a minute more before serving. Add a little water if necessary to have a light creamy consistency.

Serve with a dusting of cinnamon.

Pies

Filo pastry is the most appealing and also the most common of the many doughs used in the Middle East to make pies. In North Africa, ever-so-thin pancakes called ouarka and brik are used. You can buy these vacuum-packed in French supermarkets, but they are not here yet. Filo can be used instead. It is available in packets – frozen and vacuum-packed – and also loose. Packets vary in weight (a common weight is 400g/14oz) and in size, thinness and quality of sheets.

Little pies shaped into triangles or cigars make ideal finger foods. Because it is easy to make, I have used a largish flat square shape for individual pies to serve as a first course or main dish.

Cheese 'Cigars'

Makes 16

* 200g (7oz) feta cheese
* 1 egg, lightly beaten
* a small bunch of mint, flat-leaf parsley or dill, very finely chopped (optional)
* 4 sheets of filo pastry, or more if necessary
* 2 tablespoons melted butter or oil

The traditional Turkish filling is made with feta, but you may also like to try the cheese blend on page 56, which is delicious.

For the filling, mash the feta with a fork and mix with the egg and herbs.

Take out the sheets of filo only when you are ready to use them, as they quickly dry out. Cut the sheets into 4 rectangles about 30 × 12–13cm (12 × 4–5in) and put them in a pile on top of each other. Brush the top strip lightly with melted butter or oil. Take a heaped teaspoon of filling. Place it at one end of the strip in a thin sausage shape along the edge – about 2.5cm (1in) from it and from the side edges. Roll the strip up with the filling inside like a cigarette. Turn the ends in about a third of the way to trap the filling, then continue to roll. If the filo sheets are too thin and look likely to tear, use 2 strips together and brush with butter or oil in between.

Place the 'cigars' close to each other on a greased baking tray, brush the tops with oil or melted butter, and bake at 180°C (350°F, gas 4) for 30 minutes or until crisp and golden.

Filo Triangles with Minced Meat, Onions and Pine Nuts

Makes about 20
* 5 sheets of filo pastry, or more if necessary
* 3 tablespoons melted butter or oil

For the filling
* 1 small onion, chopped
* 2 tablespoons sunflower oil
* 250g (8oz) minced lamb or beef
* salt and pepper
* 3/4 teaspoon ground cinnamon
* 1/4 teaspoon ground allspice
* 2 tablespoons pine nuts, lightly toasted

Meat pies are traditionally made in little triangular shapes. The classic Arab filling here is called tatbila.

For the filling, fry the onion in the oil till golden. Add the meat and fry lightly, crushing it with a fork and turning it over until it changes colour, adding salt, pepper, cinnamon and allspice. Stir in the pine nuts.

Take out the sheets of filo only when you are ready to use them, as they quickly dry out. Cut the sheets into 4 rectangles about 30 × 12–13cm (12 × 4–5in) wide and put them in a pile on top of each other. Brush the top strip lightly with melted butter or oil. Take a heaped teaspoon of filling. Place it at one end of the strip of filo, about 3cm (1¼in) from the edge. Fold the end over the filling. Now pick up a corner and fold diagonally, making a triangle. Continue to fold until the whole strip has been folded into a triangular packet, making sure that you close any holes as you fold so that the filling does not ooze out. If the filo sheets are too thin and look likely to tear, use 2 strips together and brush with melted butter or oil in between.

Place the little packets close to each other on a greased baking tray, brush the tops with oil or melted butter, and bake at 180°C (350°F, gas 4) for 30 minutes or until crisp and golden.

Variations
* You can brush the pies with egg yolk and a drop of water.
* A Moroccan filling for *briouat* adds 1/4 teaspoon of ground ginger, a pinch of cayenne, 3 tablespoons of chopped coriander and 2 raw eggs to bind the meat. There are no pine nuts and they like dusting the deep-fried pies with icing sugar or ground cinnamon.

Meat Tarts

I make this version of the famous Arab sfiha *or* lahma bi agine *with frozen puff pastry. (Packets are divided into two 340g (12oz) pieces.) Serve it as an appetizer, or as a snack meal accompanied by thick strained Greek yoghurt and salad.*

Serves 3–6

* 340g (12oz) bought puff pastry, defrosted
* 1 egg white
* oil to grease the baking sheet

For the filling

* 1 onion, grated or finely chopped in the food processor and drained of its juices
* ½–1 fresh chilli pepper, finely chopped
* 350g (12oz) minced lamb
* 100g (4oz) tomato paste (³/4 of a small tin)
* 2 teaspoons sugar
* 2 tablespoons lemon juice or 1 tablespoon pomegranate concentrate
* salt and pepper

Cut the puff pastry into 6 pieces and roll each out thinly on a floured surface with a floured rolling-pin, cutting the corners so as to make rounds about 18cm (7in) in diameter. (This pastry shrinks quite a bit and will turn out much smaller when it is baked.)

Place the pastry rounds on oiled baking sheets or grease proof paper and brush the tops with egg white (this prevents the pastry getting too soggy with juice). Bake them blind in a preheated 230°C (450°F, gas 8) oven for 10 minutes until they puff up and are golden. Take them out, turn them over, brush the other side with the remaining egg white and return to the oven for another 8 minutes or until this side is crisp and lightly coloured. Let them cool.

Mix all the filling ingredients and work very well with your hands to a soft well-blended paste. Take lumps of the filling and spread thickly over each pastry round.

Place the filled tarts in the hot oven and bake for 15 minutes. Serve hot.

Variations

* Add 1 tablespoon of tamarind paste or syrup instead of lemon juice or pomegranate concentrate (if the tamarind is too hard, soften it by diluting with 1–2 tablespoons of water in a small pan over a low heat).
* Add 3 tablespoons of pine nuts to the meat mixture.
* Add 2 tablespoons of chopped parsley.
* Add 1 large tomato, peeled and chopped.

Pumpkin Pies

These Turkish pies with an unusually subtle flavour make a good first course. Middle Eastern and Oriental stores sell the orange pumpkin almost all the year round, in large slices with the seeds and stringy bits removed.

Makes 6

* 6 sheets of filo pastry
* 4 tablespoons melted butter or sunflower oil
* 1 egg yolk

For the filling

* 1kg (2lb) orange pumpkin
* 2 teaspoons sugar
* 150g (5oz) feta cheese, mashed with a fork
* 2 eggs, lightly beaten

Peel the pumpkin – and if necessary scrape off the seeds and fibrous parts. Cut it into pieces and put them into a pan with a tight-fitting lid with about 250ml (9fl oz) of water. Cook with the lid on for 20–30 minutes, until soft. Drain and mash with a potato masher or a fork. Return to the pan and leave over a high heat until all the liquid has evaporated, watching that it does not burn and stirring with a wooden spoon. The pumpkin must be quite dry. If it is wet the pastry will be soggy.

Mix with the rest of the ingredients.

Open out the sheets of filo when you are ready to make the pies and be ready to work fast. Leave the sheets in a pile and brush the top one with melted butter or oil. Put one-sixth of the filling in a mound on one side of the sheet, about 8cm (3in) from the edge, in the centre. Let it spread over a surface of about 8cm (3in).

Wrap the filling up into a flat square parcel. Fold the near edge of the sheet over the filling, then very carefully lift the filo with the filling and turn over. Continue to turn the parcel over, folding the two side ends up at different turns so that the filling ends up covered with several layers of pastry.

Continue with the remaining sheets and filling, and arrange the parcels on a sheet of foil on a baking sheet. Brush the tops with the egg yolk mixed with 1 teaspoon of water, and bake in a preheated 180°C (350°F, gas 4) oven for 35–45 minutes or until the pastry is crisp and brown.

Serve hot.

Aubergine Pies

Makes 6

* 1kg (2lb) aubergines
* 4 eggs, lightly beaten
* 150g (5oz) mature Cheddar cheese, grated
* ¼ teaspoon grated nutmeg
* salt and pepper (optional)
* 6 sheets of filo pastry
* 4 tablespoons sunflower oil or melted butter
* 1 egg yolk

These individual pies can be served as a first course or main dish. The creamy aubergine filling of Turkish inspiration is very delicate in flavour.

For the filling, grill or roast the aubergines, peel them, and chop and mash the flesh (see page 13). Mix with the eggs, cheese, nutmeg, pepper and salt (for salt take into account the saltiness of the cheese).

Open out the sheets of filo when you are ready to make the pies, and be ready to work fast. Leave the sheets in a pile and brush the top one with melted butter or oil. Put one-sixth of the filling (about 4 tablespoons) in a mound on one side of the sheet, about 8cm (3in) from the edge, in the centre. Let it spread over a surface of about 8cm (3in).

Wrap the filling up into a flat square parcel. Fold the near edge of the sheet over the filling, then very carefully lift the filo with the filling and turn over. Continue to turn the parcel over, folding the two side ends up at different turns so that the filling ends up covered with several layers of pastry.

Continue with the remaining sheets and filling, and arrange the parcels on a sheet of foil on a baking sheet. Brush the tops with the egg yolk mixed with 1 teaspoon of water, and bake in a preheated 180°C (350°F, gas 4) oven for 35–40 minutes or until the pastry is crisp and brown.

Serve hot.

Right **Cheese 'cigars'**; filo triangles with minced meat, onions and pine nuts
Overleaf **Pumpkin pies**

Seafood Pastillas

Makes 6

- 600g (1¼lb) firm white fish such as cod or haddock
- salt
- 5 tablespoons extra virgin olive oil
- juice of 1 lemon
- ½–1 teaspoon ground cumin
- 1½ teaspoons paprika
- a good pinch of chilli powder
- 2 garlic cloves, crushed
- a large bunch of flat-leaf parsley
- a large bunch of coriander
- 250g (8oz) peeled and cooked king prawns
- 6 sheets of filo pastry
- about 5 tablespoons sunflower oil
- 1 egg yolk

These Moroccan pies – made with a paper-thin dough called ouarka – can be served as a first or main course. The flavours are rich. It is important to have masses of parsley and coriander.

Poach the fish in salted water very briefly until it just begins to flake, then drain. Remove the skin and flake it into pieces.

In a bowl mix the olive oil and lemon with the cumin, paprika, chilli powder, garlic, parsley and coriander. Put in the fish and prawns and turn to cover all the pieces with this marinade.

Open out the sheets of filo when you are ready to make the pies and be ready to work fast. Leave the sheets in a pile and brush the top one with oil. Put one-sixth of the filling mixture in a flat mound on one side of the sheet, about 9cm (3½in) from the edge, in the centre. Let it spread over a surface of about 9cm (3½in).

Wrap the filling up into a flat square parcel. Fold the near edge of the sheet over the filling, then very carefully lift the filo with the filling and turn over. Continue to turn the parcel over, folding the two side ends up at different turns so that the filling ends up covered with several layers of pastry.

Continue with the remaining sheets and filling, and arrange the parcels on a sheet of foil on a baking sheet. Brush the tops with the egg yolk mixed with 1 teaspoon of water, and bake in a preheated 180°C (350°F, gas 4) oven for 35–45 minutes or until the pastry is crisp and brown.

Serve hot.

Previous page Shakshouka with peppers and tomatoes
Left Haricot bean and spinach omelette

Chicken and Onion Pies

Serves 8

* 5 large onions (about 1.5kg/3½lb)
* 4 tablespoons sunflower oil
* ½–¾ teaspoon ground ginger
* 1½ teaspoons ground cinnamon, plus more to sprinkle on at the end
* salt
* juice of ½ lemon
* 4 chicken breast fillets, skinned and boned
* a large bunch of coriander (about 100g/4oz weighed with stems), finely chopped
* 8 sheets of filo pastry
* 4–5 tablespoons melted butter or oil
* 1 egg yolk
* icing sugar (optional)

I prefer this Moroccan pie called trid *– in which the chicken is cooked in a huge mass of onions which are reduced to a creamy sauce – to the more famous* pastilla *with eggs. It is light and tasty and makes a grand party dish.*

Chop the onions in batches in the food processor. Put them into a large saucepan with the oil, ginger, cinnamon, a little salt and lemon juice and the chicken fillets. Put the lid on and cook on a low heat for about 15 minutes.

Take out the chicken pieces and continue cooking the onions without the lid on so that the liquid evaporates. Cook until the onions have been reduced to a creamy sauce and you can see the oil sizzling – it takes about 1 hour – stirring every so often.

Cut the chicken into smallish pieces and put them back into the pan with the onion sauce. Add the coriander and mix very well. Taste and add salt and more of the flavourings if necessary.

Open out the sheets of filo when you are ready to use them and be ready to work fast as they dry out. Leave them in a pile. Brush the top one with melted butter or oil.

Take about one-eighth of the chicken and onion mixture and put it in a flat mound on the sheet about 8cm (3in) from one edge, in the middle. Fold the edge over the filling, and turn the packet over with the filling, folding the side ends of the sheet up at different turns so as to end up with a flat parcel with several layers of pastry on either side.

Continue with the rest of the filo sheets and filling, and place all the parcels on a sheet of foil on a baking dish or tray. Brush the tops with the egg yolk mixed with 1 teaspoon of water. Bake in a preheated 180°C (350°F, gas 4) oven for 35–45 minutes, until crisp and golden.

Serve hot. Pass round little pots of icing sugar and cinnamon for everyone to sprinkle on if they wish.

Variation
* Another Moroccan pie has a filling of chicken mixed with 1 fried chopped onion, 250g (8oz) of boiled and mashed potatoes, some chopped flat-leaf parsley, 2 chopped hard-boiled eggs and 2 raw eggs (as a binder). It is served hot with lemon wedges.

Spinach Pies with Raisins and Pine Nuts

Serves 4

* 4 sheets of filo pastry or more if necessary
* 2 tablespoons melted butter or oil
* 1 egg yolk

For the filling

* 1lb (500g) spinach
* 1 medium onion, chopped
* 4 tablespoons extra virgin olive oil
* salt and pepper
* 2 tablespoons pine nuts, lightly toasted
* 2 tablespoons raisins

Serve these as a first course.

Wash the spinach and remove only stems which are thick and tough, then drain. Put the leaves into a large pan with the lid on. Cook over a low heat until they crumple into a soft mass (they steam in the water that clings to them). Drain and press all the water out, as it would make the pastry soggy. Then slice.

Fry the onion in 2 tablespoons of the oil till golden. Add the spinach, season with salt and pepper and cook over a high heat to evaporate any remaining liquid. Stir in the pine nuts and raisins.

Open out the sheets of filo when you are ready to make the pies and be ready to work fast. Leave the sheets in a pile and brush the top one with oil. Put a quarter of the filling in a flat mound on one side of the sheet, about 8cm (3in) from the edge, in the centre.

Wrap the filling up into a square parcel. Fold the near edge of the sheet over the filling, then very carefully lift the filo with the filling and turn over. Continue to turn the parcel over, folding the two side ends up at different turns so that the filling ends up covered with several layers of pastry.

Continue with the remaining sheets and filling, and arrange the parcels on a sheet of foil on a baking sheet. Brush the tops with the egg yolk mixed with 1 teaspoon of water, and bake in a preheated 180°C (350°F, gas 4) oven for 35–45 minutes or until the pastry is crisp and brown.

Serve hot.

Variation

* Before serving, dust the tops with a little icing sugar and ground cinnamon.

Large Spinach Pie in a Tray

Makes 16–20

* 1kg (2lb) fresh spinach
* 125g (4¹/₂oz) feta cheese
* 125g (4¹/₂oz) cottage cheese
* 4 eggs, lightly beaten
* a bunch of dill, finely chopped (optional)
* ¹/₄ teaspoon grated nutmeg
* salt and pepper
* 1 packet of filo pastry
* 100g (4oz) butter, melted, or about 100ml (4fl oz) olive or sunflower oil

This is the Greek spanakopitta.

Wash the spinach and cut off any hard stems, then drain. Put the leaves in a pan and cook with the lid on and no extra water for minutes only, until they crumple into a soft mass. They steam in the water that clings to them. Drain and press out the excess liquid, which could make the pastry soggy. Return the spinach to the pan and dry it out further over a high heat.

Mash the cheeses together with a fork. Add the eggs, spinach, dill, nutmeg, salt if necessary (take into account the saltiness of the cheese) and pepper.

Follow the instructions for **Making a large layered filo pie in a tray** below.

Serve hot.

Making a large layered filo pie in a tray

Use a large baking dish or tray, a little smaller than the filo sheets. Brush it with oil or melted butter. Place 7 sheets of filo (about half the packet), one on top of the other, over the bottom of the tray, brushing each sheet with oil or melted butter and letting the sheets come up along the sides.

Spread the filling evenly on top. Then cover with the remaining sheets, brushing each, including the top one, with oil or melted butter.

With a sharp pointed knife, cut into 5cm (2in) squares or diamonds with parallel lines only down to the filling, not right through.

Bake at 180°C (350°F, gas 4) for 45 minutes or until crisp and golden. Cut along the cutting lines, this time right through to the bottom, and serve hot.

Large Cheese Pie

Makes 16–20

* 250g (8oz) Edam cheese
* 250g (8oz) Gouda cheese
* 250g (8oz) Cheddar cheese
* 250g (8oz) cottage cheese
* 4 eggs, lightly beaten
* 1 packet of filo pastry
* 150g (5oz) melted butter or sunflower oil
* 1 egg yolk, to glaze

The traditional filling for the Greek tyropitta *is made with feta cheese. This milder-tasting alternative, which my contemporaries from Egypt adopted in Britain, can be served as a teatime savoury or main course.*

Put the cheeses (cut into large pieces) with the eggs in the food processor and blend to a homogeneous mass.

Follow the instructions for **Making a large layered filo pie in a tray** on page 55.

Serve hot.

Variations

* Add 3 tablespoons of finely chopped dill or mint to the filling, and 1/4 teaspoon of grated nutmeg.
* Paint the top sheet of pastry with 1 egg yolk mixed with 1 teaspoon of water (do not brush with butter) and sprinkle with sesame seeds.
* For an alternative filling mix 500g (1lb) of cottage cheese with 500g (1lb) of feta (both drained of their liquid), 4 eggs, pepper and 4 tablespoons of finely chopped dill, chervil, chives or flat-leaf parsley.

Creamy Cheese Pie

Serves 6–8

* 200g (7oz) feta cheese
* 200g (7oz) cottage or curd cheese
* a large bunch of dill, finely chopped (optional)
* 75g (3oz) butter, melted
* ½ litre (17fl oz) milk, warmed
* 4 eggs, lightly beaten
* 7 sheets of filo pastry (about 200g/7oz)
* 200g (7oz) Turkish kaşar or mature Cheddar cheese, grated

I discovered this wonderful filo pie, which is more like a custardy flan, called tepsi böreği, *in Turkey. It sounds complicated but it is quite easy and you will be delighted by the lightness and the variety of flavours and textures.*

For the filling, blend the feta with the cottage or curd cheese and dill (if using).

Mix the melted butter, milk and eggs and beat well.

Use a rectangular baking dish about 25 × 36cm (10 × 14in). Open the sheets only when you are ready to use them and keep them in a pile so that they do not dry out.

Lay a sheet in the greased baking dish, folding it and fitting it into the corners. With a ladle, pour a little of the butter, milk and egg mixture (about $^1/_7$ as you will need enough to pour over 7) all over the sheet, then sprinkle with the grated kasar or Cheddar.

Do the same with a second and third sheet.

Lay the fourth sheet on top and spread the filling evenly on top. (It is easier to make many little blobs of filling.) Cover with the remaining sheets, ladling some of the butter, milk and egg mixture over each one (including the last) and sprinkling with the grated kaşar or Cheddar. Fold the last sheet so that the folded bit is underneath and it presents a smooth surface.

Bake at 180°C (350°F, gas 4) oven for 35–45 minutes, until the top is golden brown. It puffs up and falls again when you cut it.

Serve hot, cut into squares.

Eggs

Egg dishes are popular in the Middle East as a light main meal. They also make a good first course.

Poached Eggs with Yoghurt

Serves 2

* 1 tablespoon vinegar
* salt
* 4 tablespoons thick strained Greek yoghurt, at room temperature
* 1 small garlic clove, crushed (optional)
* 1 tablespoon butter
* ½ teaspoon paprika
* 2 eggs

This is the Turkish çilbir. *You can do the same with fried eggs.*

Put enough water into a pan to cover the eggs. Add the vinegar and salt, bring to the boil, then reduce the heat to lowest.

Beat the yoghurt with the garlic. Melt the butter with the paprika.

Break each egg into a cup and slide them into the pan of water. Cook for 1–2 minutes until the whites have set. Lift out with a perforated spoon. Serve at once.

Sprinkle with a little salt, pour 2 tablespoons of yoghurt over each egg, and dribble butter and paprika over the yoghurt.

Fried Eggs with Halumi Cheese

Serves 2

* 2 thick slices of halumi cheese
* 2 tablespoons butter or
  sunflower oil
* 2 eggs
* salt and pepper

This dish is traditionally prepared in individual portions in two-handled frying pans and served in the same pans straight from the fire, but you can, of course, use one large frying pan.

Fry the cheese in hot butter or oil over a medium heat. When it begins to soften, open the egg over it and continue to cook until the white has set.

Sprinkle lightly with salt (taking into account the saltiness of the cheese) and pepper, and serve very hot.

Tomatoes and Eggs

Serves 4

* 2 garlic cloves, crushed
* 1 tablespoon olive oil
* 500g (1lb) tomatoes, peeled and chopped
* ½ teaspoon ground cinnamon
* 1 teaspoon sugar
* salt and pepper
* 2 sprigs of mint or a small bunch of flat-leaf parsley, chopped
* 4 eggs

In a large frying pan, heat the garlic in the oil, then add the tomatoes, cinnamon, sugar, salt and pepper.

Cook for 10–15 minutes, then stir in the mint or parsley. Break each egg into a cup and slide them whole into the sauce. Cook until the eggs are set.

Variation

* You may stir the eggs a little to have a creamy scramble.

Onion and Herb Omelette

Serves 2

* 1 large onion, coarsely chopped
* 3 tablespoons sunflower oil
* 2 eggs, lightly beaten
* a good bunch of flat-leaf parsley, chopped
* a good bunch of coriander, chopped
* a sprig of fresh mint, finely chopped
* salt and pepper

Fry the onion in 2 tablespoons of the oil till soft and golden. Mix with the eggs and the other ingredients.

Heat the remaining oil in a preferably non-stick frying pan. Pour in the egg mixture and cook over a medium heat. As soon as the bottom sets, put under the grill and cook the other side until the top is firm and brown.

Serve hot or cold.

Variation

* You can do tiny omelettes like little pancakes to serve as finger food. Pour them by the tablespoon into the frying pan and turn over to brown the other side. Do them in batches.

Aubergine Omelette

Serves 2

* 2 aubergines (about 500kg/1lb)
* 2 eggs, lightly beaten
* salt and pepper
* a pinch of grated nutmeg
* 1 tablespoon sunflower oil

This can be served hot or cold and makes a good mezze or first course.

Roast the aubergines under the grill, then peel and mash them (see page 13).

Beat the mashed aubergine with the eggs, season with salt and pepper and add nutmeg.

Heat the oil in a preferably non-stick frying pan and pour in the egg mixture. Cook for a few minutes on a low heat until the bottom begins to set and feels loose when you shake the pan. Continue to cook under the grill until the top is firm and lightly coloured. Alternatively turn the omelette over by slipping it first on to a plate.

Courgette Omelette

Serves 2

* 1 large onion, chopped
* 3 tablespoons olive oil
* 2 largish courgettes, cut in half lengthwise and then into slices
* salt and pepper
* 4 eggs, lightly beaten

Fry the onion in 2 tablespoons of the oil until lightly coloured.

Add the courgettes and sauté, stirring, for a minute or two. Season with salt and pepper, add about 120ml (4fl oz) of water, and cook with a lid on until the courgettes are just tender. Remove the lid and keep over a high heat to evaporate the water. Mix with the eggs and add a little salt and pepper.

Heat the remaining oil in a preferably non-stick frying pan and pour in the egg mixture. Cook over a medium heat until the bottom sets. Then put under the grill.

Serve hot or cold.

Potato and Parsley Omelette

Serves 4

* 500kg (1lb) floury potatoes, peeled
* salt
* 1 large onion, chopped
* 3 tablespoons sunflower or olive oil
* 3 eggs, lightly beaten
* a large bunch of flat-leaf parsley, chopped
* pepper

This is a Tunisian maacouda.

Boil the potatoes in salted water, then drain and mash them. Fry the onion in 2 tablespoons of the oil till soft and golden, stirring occasionally. Beat the eggs into the potatoes and add the fried onions, parsley, salt and pepper.

Heat the remaining oil in a preferably non-stick frying pan and pour in the potato mixture. Cook, covered, over a low heat until the bottom sets. Then put it under the grill to cook the top until lightly coloured.

Serve hot or cold.

Artichoke Omelette

Serves 2

* 200g (7oz) frozen artichoke
  bottoms, defrosted
* salt
* 4 eggs, lightly beaten
* pepper
* 1 garlic clove, crushed
* a few sprigs of dill, finely
  chopped
* a squeeze of lemon juice
* 1–2 tablespoons olive oil

This is an elegant and tasty omelette. It is good served with yoghurt. Use the frozen artichoke bottoms from Egypt which you can find in Middle Eastern stores.

Boil the artichoke bottoms in salted water for a few minutes until soft, then drain. Chop and mash them.

Mix the eggs with salt and pepper, the garlic, dill and lemon juice, then beat in the artichokes.

Heat the oil in a preferably non-stick frying pan, pour in the egg mixture and cook over a low heat with the lid on until the bottom sets. Then put under the grill and cook the top until slightly coloured.

Serve hot or cold.

Haricot Bean and Spinach Omelette

Serves 4

* 250g (8oz) spinach
* 1 onion, chopped
* 2 tablespoons olive oil
* 2 teaspoons tomato paste
* 3 eggs
* 1 × 420g (15oz) tin of haricot or cannellini beans, drained (yields 200g/7oz beans)
* 65g (2½oz) Gruyère cheese, grated
* salt and pepper

In Tunisia, where they use eggs more than anywhere else, they call this a tagine *because it is cooked in a clay dish of that name. It can be eaten hot or cold.*

Wash the spinach and remove the stalks only if they are thick and tough. Put the leaves into a large pan over a low heat with the lid on and only the water that clings to them. They will crumple into a soft mass within a minute. Drain and squeeze all the water out in a colander, then cut the spinach into ribbons.

Fry the onion in 1 tablespoon of olive oil until golden, then stir in the tomato paste.

Lightly beat the eggs in a bowl. Add the spinach, onions, drained beans and Gruyère, season with salt and pepper and mix well.

Heat the remaining oil in a preferably non-stick frying pan and pour the mixture in. Cook over a low heat with the lid on for 8–10 minutes, until the eggs set at the bottom. Then put under the grill to dry the top.

Shakshouka with Peppers and Tomatoes

Serves 4
- 2 red or green peppers, cut into ribbons
- 3 tablespoons sunflower or extra virgin olive oil
- 3–4 garlic cloves, sliced
- 4 medium tomatoes, peeled and cut in quarters
- salt and pepper
- 4 eggs

In a large frying pan over a medium heat fry the peppers in the oil, stirring and turning them over until they soften. Add the garlic and when it just begins to colour, add the tomatoes and salt. Cook until the tomatoes soften.

Break each egg into a cup and slide them whole into the sauce. Season again with salt and pepper, and cook until they set. Alternatively, you may stir the eggs gently and cook until creamy.

Serve hot with bread.

Variation
- In Tunisia they may add ½ teaspoon of harissa (see page 171) and 1 teaspoon of caraway seeds, or the peel of 1 preserved lemon (see page 84), cut into pieces, and 2 tablespoons of capers.

Shakshouka with Merguez

Serves 4

* 8 merguez
* 3 tablespoons extra virgin olive oil
* 3–4 garlic cloves, chopped
* 500g (1lb) tomatoes, peeled and chopped
* salt and pepper
* 4 eggs

Merguez are spicy North African sausages.

Fry the sausages in the oil, turning them over, for 1–2 minutes. Add the garlic, and when the aroma rises, add the tomatoes. Sprinkle with salt and pepper and cook for about 15 minutes until the sauce is reduced a little.

Break in the eggs and let them cook, whole, in the sauce. Serve hot with bread.

Variation

* In Tunisia they add ½–1 teaspoon of harissa (see page 171) to the tomato sauce.

Courgette Gratin

Serves 6–8

* 1 large onion, chopped
* 2 tablespoons sunflower oil
* 1kg (2lb) courgettes, cut into 1cm (½in) slices
* salt
* 3 eggs, lightly beaten
* 250g (8oz) Cheddar cheese, grated
* pepper
* a pinch of grated nutmeg

This is a family dish my mother served with yoghurt.

Soften the onion in the oil. Poach the courgettes in salted water for a few minutes until just tender and drain. Mix with the onions in an ovenproof dish.

Mix the eggs and cheese and add pepper and nutmeg. Pour over the vegetables.

Bake in a preheated 180°C (350°F, gas 4) oven for about 25 minutes or until lightly browned.

Fish   I am often told when I am given a recipe and I ask what fish to use: 'Any fish will do.' So feel free, as I do, to substitute. Most of the Mediterranean fish – sea bass, sea bream, sole, gurnard, John Dory, red mullet, hake and tuna – are easy to obtain, but you can use fish from other seas, such as cod, haddock, halibut and snapper. The usual way of cooking fish in the Middle East is to grill it, or to dip it in flour and deep-fry, and the usual dressing is lemon juice and a dribble of olive oil, but there are also some wonderful special recipes.

Marinated Fish

Serves 8

* 1kg (2lb) fish fillets, skinned and cut into 4cm (1½in) pieces
* flour
* olive oil or sunflower oil for frying

For the marinade

* a large bunch of coriander, chopped
* 1 onion, finely chopped
* 1 fresh chilli pepper, finely chopped
* 2 garlic cloves, crushed
* 6–8 tablespoons extra virgin olive oil
* juice of ½–1 lemon
* salt

This makes an excellent first course or cold buffet dish. The fish is first fried then marinated in a dressing. Make it at least an hour before you are ready to serve. You can use fish such as bream, cod or haddock.

Dip the fish fillets in flour, turning to cover them lightly all over. Shallow-fry them briefly in hot oil till golden, turning them over once. Drain on kitchen paper.

Mix the marinade ingredients and turn the fish in this mixture.

Leave for at least an hour before serving cold.

Cold Poached Fish with Lemony Pine Nut Sauce

Serves 6
* 6 fish steaks or fillets
* salt

For the tarator sauce
* 1 slice of white bread, crusts removed
* 175g (6oz) pine nuts
* juice of 1–2 lemons, to taste
* 1–2 garlic cloves, crushed
* salt and white pepper
* 120ml (4fl oz) light sesame or sunflower oil

The sharp, garlicky pine nut sauce called tarator *gives cold fish a certain grandeur. At buffet parties in Syria and Lebanon a whole fish is covered with it and decorated as with mayonnaise. You may use any white fish – fillets or steaks.*

Poach the fish in gently simmering salted water for 3–6 minutes, depending on the thickness and type of fish, until the flesh begins to flake when you cut into it. Lift out with a slotted spoon.

For the sauce, soak the bread in water and squeeze dry. Put it in the food processor with the pine nuts, lemon juice and garlic, a little salt and pepper, and enough oil to give a cream the consistency of mayonnaise.

Variation
* Add $1/4$ teaspoon of turmeric or a pinch of powdered saffron to the poaching water.

Fish Kebab

Serves 4

* 600g (1¼lb) fish, cut into 3cm (1¼in) cubes
* bay leaves
* 1 medium onion
* 6 tablespoons extra virgin olive oil
* juice of ½ lemon
* salt and pepper
* 1 lemon, cut in wedges, to serve

In Turkey swordfish is the usual fish for kebabs, but you can use any firm-fleshed white fish.

Thread the fish cubes on to wooden or flat wide metal skewers, alternating with bay leaves.

Liquidize the onion in the blender with the oil, lemon, salt and pepper and marinate the fish on the skewers in this mixture for 20 minutes, leaving it, covered, in the refrigerator.

Cook over glowing embers or under the grill for 4–6 minutes, turning the skewers a few times and brushing with the marinade.

Serve with lemon wedges.

Grilled Tuna with Tomato and Caper Dressing

Serves 4

* 8 tablespoons mild extra virgin olive oil
* 4 tuna steaks
* salt and pepper
* juice of 1 lemon
* 2 tomatoes, diced
* 2 tablespoons capers, soaked to remove excess salt or vinegar

The best way of eating tuna is seared on the outside and raw on the inside, which makes it deliciously meltingly tender. Otherwise it quickly dries out. It can be brushed with oil and cooked on the barbecue or under the grill, but an easy and perfect way is to do it in a heavy pan just filmed with oil. The dressing is a glamorized version of the ubiquitous oil and lemon one. Use it for other fish too.

Heat 2 tablespoons of the oil in a heavy frying pan. Put in the tuna steaks and cook over a high heat for 1–2 minutes on either side, depending on their thickness. You should see the flesh still dark inside as it pales on the outside.

For the dressing, mix the rest of the ingredients with the remaining olive oil. Heat through to not quite boiling point and pour over the fish as you serve it.

Variation

* Add a bunch of coriander, finely chopped, or 2 crushed garlic cloves and 1/4–1/2 teaspoon of harissa (see page 171) to the dressing.

Red Mullet Wrapped in Vine Leaves

Serves 6

* 6 red mullet (about 200g/7oz each)
* 12 vine leaves
* extra virgin olive oil
* salt
* 1½ lemons, cut in wedges, to serve

Vine leaves keep the fish moist and impart a delicate flavour. This dish is simple to make and beautiful to offer at a dinner party. You may use fresh or preserved leaves. If the vine leaves are fresh, scald them in boiling water for a moment or two until they flop, then dip them in cold water. If they are preserved in brine, soak them in hot water to remove the salt and rinse them. You can now easily buy vine leaves in brine. You can keep those you haven't used in a jar, covered with water with plenty of salt.

Ask the fishmonger to clean and scale the fish and to keep the heads on.

Place two vine leaves on a plate, shiny side down, and brush with oil. Place a fish across the leaves. Sprinkle with salt and roll up into a parcel, folding the top leaf so that the head sticks out. Repeat with the remaining fish and leaves.

Cook on a barbecue or under the grill for about 4–5 minutes on each side.

Serve with lemon wedges.

Variation

* Use sardines instead of red mullet.
* Stuff the fish with a mixture of 3 crushed garlic cloves and plenty of chopped flat-leaf parsley with a little salt and pepper.

Deep-fried Fish

Deep-frying is the most popular way of cooking medium-sized whole fish as well as fish steaks and fillets in the Arab world.

Season the fish with salt inside and out and cover entirely, but lightly, with flour. Fish steaks or fillets can be further dipped in lightly beaten egg for extra protection.

It is best to use olive oil, which can reach high temperatures without deteriorating. Heat the oil in a large saucepan so that there is no risk of the oil bubbling over and use enough to cover the fish – it can be filtered and re-used.

Put the fish in when the oil sizzles when you throw in a piece of bread. Then keep the oil at a constant – not too high – temperature so that the fish has time to cook inside before the skin gets burnt. Turn the fish over once and give it about 3 minutes on each side. Lift out and drain on kitchen paper.

Serve accompanied by lemon wedges and, if you like, a sauce such as *chermoula* (page 82) or *tarator* (page 75).

Fried Fish Balls

Makes about 50

* 1kg (2lb) minced fish or skinned fillets
* 2 eggs
* 2 teaspoons salt
* ½ teaspoon pepper
* 2 teaspoons ground cumin
* 2–4 garlic cloves, crushed
* 75g (3oz) fine breadcrumbs or matzo meal
* a bunch of flat-leaf parsley or coriander, finely chopped (optional)
* flour
* oil for deep-frying

You can serve these Egyptian fish balls as finger foods at a party. Use fish such as cod, haddock, bream, whiting or hake. You can buy mixed minced fish at some fishmongers. Otherwise buy skinned fish fillets and put them briefly through the food processor.

If using fish fillets, cut them into pieces and finely chop them in the food processor for 5 seconds only.

Beat the eggs lightly and add salt, pepper, cumin and garlic. Mix with the fish and add the breadcrumbs or matzo meal and the parsley. Work very well into a paste with your hands.

Wet your hands, take lumps of paste, and roll them into balls the size of large marbles. Pour a good amount of flour on to a plate and roll the fish balls in it, covering them lightly with flour.

Deep-fry briefly in hot oil until browned all over, turning them over once.

Drain on kitchen paper and serve, preferably hot.

Roast Fish with Lemon and Honeyed Onion

Serves 4

* 2 whole sea bass or bream (about 500g/1lb each)
* 2 tablespoons olive oil
* salt and pepper
* juice of ½ lemon
* 1 lemon, cut into wedges, to garnish

For the honeyed onion

* 500g (1lb) onions, cut in half and sliced
* 4 tablespoons extra virgin olive oil
* 2 tablespoons honey
* juice of ½ lemon
* salt and pepper

Cook the onions in the oil on a very low heat, with the lid on, stirring occasionally, until very soft. Then remove the lid and cook, stirring, until the onions are golden.

Add the honey, lemon juice, salt and pepper, and cook for another 5 minutes. Reheat when ready to serve.

Brush the fish with 1 tablespoon of the oil and season lightly with salt and pepper. Place in a baking dish with a mixture of lemon juice and the remaining oil.

Bake for 15–20 minutes in a preheated 190°C (375°F, gas 5) oven, or until done, then put under the grill for 2 minutes, until the skin is crisp and brown. Serve with the honeyed onions, garnished with lemon wedges.

Variation

* Add 2 tablespoons of raisins or sultanas to the onion while it is cooking.

Pan-cooked Fish with Chermoula

Serves 4

* a large bunch of coriander, chopped
* 4 garlic cloves, crushed
* $1/2$–1 teaspoon ground cumin
* 1 teaspoon paprika
* $1/4$–$1/2$ teaspoon chilli powder (optional)
* 6 tablespoons groundnut or extra virgin olive oil
* juice of 1 lemon or 3 tablespoons wine vinegar
* 1kg (2lb) fish fillets, such as bream, turbot and hake (keep the skin on)

The hot spicy chermoula is the all-purpose Moroccan marinade and sauce used with every kind of fish – fried, grilled, baked and stewed.

For the *chermoula*, blend everything except the fish together in the food processor.

Marinate the fish in half the sauce for 30 minutes – keeping the rest aside.

Cook the fish in a large non-stick frying pan filmed with oil, over a medium heat. Put the fillets in, skin side down, and cook, turning them over once, for about 8–10 minutes or until done to your liking.

Serve with the remaining sauce poured over.

Variation
* Grill the fish skin side only towards the heat.

Right **Marinated fish**
Overleaf **Fish kebab; rice with herbs**

Fish with Preserved Lemon, Green Olives, and Capers

Serves 4

* 2 tablespoons butter
* 2 tablespoons groundnut or extra virgin olive oil
* 1/3 teaspoon ground ginger
* 1/4 teaspoon powdered saffron
* 4 fish steaks or escalopes, such as bream or turbot
* salt and pepper
* 1/2–1 preserved lemon (see page 84), rinsed and cut into small pieces
* 12 green olives
* 2 tablespoons capers, soaked to remove their excess salt or vinegar
* a good bunch of coriander leaves, chopped

In a large frying pan heat the butter with the oil and stir in the ginger and saffron.

Put in the fish. Sprinkle with salt and pepper and add the preserved lemon, olives, capers and coriander. Cook for 6–10 minutes, turning the fish over once.

Previous page Red mullet in a hot saffron and ginger tomato sauce
Left Chicken with tomatoes and honey

Preserved lemons

Preserved lemons lend a distinctive flavour to North African dishes. They take about 4 weeks to mature and can keep for a year. Only the skin is used – the pulp is scooped out and thrown away. You can use small limes with thin skins or ordinary lemons with thick ones.

There are three common ways of making them. I am especially fond of a quick unorthodox method (3) which gives delicious results in 4 days.

1. Lemons preserved in salt and lemon juice

In this method, considered most prestigious, no water is used. 65g (2½oz) of salt is required for 500g (1lb) of lemons. This works out at about 75g (3oz) or 4 tablespoons of salt for 4 lemons.

* 4 lemons (choose them with thick skins)
* 4 tablespoons sea salt
* juice of 4 more lemons or more

Wash and scrub the lemons. The classic Moroccan way is to cut each lemon in quarters but not right through, so that the pieces are still attached at the stem end, and to stuff each with plenty of salt. Put them into a glass jar, pressing them down so that they are squashed together, and close the jar. Leave for 3–4 days, by which time the lemons will have released some of their juices and the skins will have softened a little. Press them down as much as you can and add fresh lemon juice to cover them entirely. Close the jar and leave in a cool place for at least a month, by which time the lemons should be ready. The longer they are left the better the flavour. (If a piece of lemon is not covered it develops a white mould which is harmless and just needs to be washed off.)

Before using, rinse to get rid of the salt.

2. Lemons pickled in brine

This is the same procedure as above, but instead of adding lemon juice, cover the lemons with brine, adding 2 tablespoons of salt to the warm water. Lemons prepared this way take longer to mature. Some people pour a little oil on top as a protective film.

3. Lemons boiled in brine and preserved in oil

With a sharp knife make 8 fine – superficial, not deep – incisions into the lemon skin from one end of the lemon to the other. Put the lemons in a large pan with salted water (the same proportion of salt as above – for instance 8 tablespoons for 8 lemons) to cover. Put a smaller lid on top of them to keep them down as they float, and boil for about 25 minutes or until the peels are very soft. When cool enough to handle, scoop out the flesh, pack the skins into a glass jar and cover with sunflower or light vegetable oil.

Red Mullet in a Hot Saffron and Ginger Tomato Sauce

Serves 4

* 4 red mullet (about 1kg/2lb)
* 3 garlic cloves, chopped
* 1 fresh chilli pepper, finely chopped
* 2–3 tablespoons extra virgin olive oil
* 500g (1lb) ripe tomatoes, peeled and chopped
* salt and pepper
* 1½ teaspoons sugar
* ¼ teaspoon saffron pistils
* 3cm (1¼in) fresh root ginger, grated or crushed in a garlic press to extract the juice

The sauce is splendid. You can use fillet of fish such as bream, if you like, instead of the mullet.

Have the fish scaled and cleaned but leave the heads on and keep the livers, which are a delicacy.

In a frying pan heat the garlic and the chilli pepper in the oil for moments only until they soften. Add the tomatoes, salt, pepper, sugar, saffron and ginger and simmer for 15 minutes.

Put in the fish with their livers replaced in the cavities, and simmer for 10–12 minutes or until done, turning them over once.

Poached Fish with Saffron Vermicelli

Serves 4

* 600g (1¼lb) fish
* salt and pepper
* 300g (10oz) vermicelli
* ½ teaspoon powdered saffron
* 4–5 tablespoons extra virgin olive oil
* a bunch of flat-leaf parsley or coriander, chopped

For this North African dish, use fish fillets – monkfish or any firm-fleshed fish such as bream, turbot, cod, haddock – and have them skinned.

Poach the fish in barely simmering salted water for 5–10 minutes until the flesh looks opaque when you cut into it.

At the same time break the vermicelli in your hand into little pieces and cook in about 1.2 litres (2 pints) of boiling salted water with the saffron until just tender, stirring vigorously so that the vermicelli do not stick together. Drain, reserving about 150ml (¼ pint) of the saffron water to use as a sauce. Beat in the olive oil, some salt and pepper and the parsley or coriander.

Serve the fish on a bed of vermicelli, with the sauce poured over.

Couscous with Seafood and a Fresh Tomato Sauce

Serves 4

* 400g (14oz) couscous
* 3 garlic cloves, finely chopped
* 2 tablespoons extra virgin olive oil
* 750g (1½lb) large ripe tomatoes, peeled and chopped
* salt and pepper
* 2 teaspoons sugar
* 2½cm (1in) fresh root ginger, grated or crushed in a garlic press to extract the juice
* a pinch of chilli flakes or chilli powder (optional)
* 400g (14oz) tin of chickpeas, drained
* 2 tablespoons raisins (optional)
* 500g (1lb) fish steaks or escalopes, skinned (use cod, bream, hake)
* 250g (8oz) cooked and shelled king prawns
* a large bunch of flat-leaf parsley, finely chopped
* a large bunch of coriander, finely chopped

Prepare the couscous as described on page 168, using the same volume of water as the grain – that is, about 475ml (16fl oz).

Sweat the garlic in the oil for a few seconds. Add the tomatoes, salt, pepper, sugar, ginger, chilli, chickpeas and raisins, and simmer for 15 minutes.

Put in the fish and cook for 5–10 minutes or until the flesh flakes when you cut into it. Add the prawns, parsley and coriander and cook through.

Serve hot, poured over the hot couscous.

Variations

* For a hot Tunisian version add 1 teaspoon of harissa (see page 171) to the sauce and omit the chilli.
* Garnish with 8 green or black olives.
* A lovely version is made with quince. Peel, core and slice 1 quince and throw into the sauce. Simmer until the slices are tender before adding the fish.

Prawn and Tomato Pilaf

Serves 6–8

* 750g (1½lb) tomatoes
* 1 large onion, chopped
* 3 tablespoons extra virgin olive oil
* 4 garlic cloves, chopped
* ½ fresh chilli pepper, finely chopped
* 2 chicken stock cubes
* 400g (14oz) American long-grain rice
* salt and pepper
* 2 teaspoons sugar
* 1 teaspoon ground cinnamon
* 600g (1¼lb) peeled cooked tiger or king prawns
* 2 lemons, cut into quarters, to serve

This can be served as a first course or main dish. It has a deliciously fresh tomato flavour with a touch of cinnamon.

Peel the tomatoes and liquidize them in the food processor, then measure their volume. It should add up to a little more than 500ml (18fl oz).

Fry the onion in the oil till soft and lightly coloured. Add the garlic and chilli pepper and stir until the aroma rises.

Add the liquidized tomatoes and just enough water to make up 1 litre (1³/4 pints) with the tomatoes. Stir in the crumbled stock cubes and bring to the boil. Add the rice, salt and pepper, sugar and cinnamon. Stir well and cook, covered, on a low heat for about 20 minutes. The rice should be tender but still a little moist. Fold in the prawns gently and heat through with the lid on.

Serve hot, accompanied by lemon wedges.

Spicy King Prawns

Serves 2

* 2 garlic cloves, crushed
* 3 tablespoons sunflower or extra virgin olive oil
* 1 teaspoon paprika
* 3/4 teaspoon ground cumin
* 1/4 teaspoon ground ginger
* a good pinch of cayenne
* 250g (8oz) king prawns, peeled and cooked
* salt
* a large bunch of fresh coriander or flat-leaf parsley, chopped

This is a Moroccan way with prawns – quick to do and delicious.

Heat the garlic in the oil until the aroma rises. Stir in the spices and throw in the prawns. Season with salt, add the coriander or parsley, and fry quickly, stirring for a minute or so to heat through.

Scallops with Tamarind

Serves 4
* 1 tablespoon tamarind paste
* 3 tablespoons water
* 4 tablespoons mild extra virgin olive oil
* 12 scallops
* salt

You can buy tamarind paste from Indian and Middle Eastern stores.

In a little pan heat the tamarind and water, stirring, until the tamarind dissolves, and let it cool. Then beat in the oil.

Wash the scallops and pull away the intestinal thread. Cook them in a greased frying pan for 30–40 seconds on each side, sprinkling with a little salt.

Serve hot with a drizzle of dressing on each.

Variation
* Serve with a mixture of 3 tablespoons of extra virgin olive oil and 1 teaspoon of ground cinnamon instead of the tamarind dressing.

Octopus Cooked in White Wine

Serves 6

* 1 small octopus, (about 1kg/2lb)
* 200ml (7fl oz) white wine
* 2 tablespoons white wine vinegar
* 2 teaspoons sugar
* salt and pepper
* 5–6 tablespoons olive oil
* a bunch of flat-leaf parsley, chopped

This is served as an appetizer in Greece. The wine gives it a delicious flavour.

Octopus is sold cleaned and tenderized. Cut part way through the muscle which unites the tentacles to the inside of the head and discard all the contents of the head cavity. This involves pulling or cutting out the ink sac, the hard oval 'beak' and the gelatinous innards. Turn the head inside out and wash well under running water. Squeeze or cut out the eyes and any cartilage. Remove any scales which may be left on the suckers and wash the octopus thoroughly.

Blanch the octopus for 5 minutes in boiling water, then drain. Put it into a saucepan with the wine, vinegar, sugar, salt and pepper and just enough water to cover. Simmer over a very low heat for about 1–1^{1}/$_{2}$ hours until tender, adding water as required, and letting the sauce reduce when the octopus is done.

Cut into 2.5cm (1in) slices and mix with the cooking juices and the olive oil.

Serve cold, sprinkled with parsley.

Squid with Garlic and Chillies

Serves 4

* 750g (1½lb) small squid
* 3 tablespoons olive oil
* 3 garlic cloves, chopped
* 2 fresh red chilli peppers, seeded and finely chopped
* salt and pepper
* a bunch of coriander, chopped
* 1 lemon, cut in wedges, to serve

To clean and prepare the squid, pull the head away from the body pouch and discard the soft innards which come out with it. Discard the remaining insides of the pouch – the ink sac, if any, the icicle-shaped transparent cuttlebone and the soft innards. Keep the tentacles in their bunches but remove the eyes and the small round cartilage at the base of the tentacles by cutting with a sharp knife just above the eyes (be careful that ink doesn't squirt out at you from the eyes). Rinse thoroughly. Cut the body pouches in rings.

Heat the oil in a large frying pan. Put in the garlic and chilli peppers and the squid. Season with salt and pepper and sauté briefly, turning over the pieces, for 2–3 minutes only.

Sprinkle with coriander and serve hot, with lemon wedges.

Poultry

Chicken is popular food, and pigeons, quails and ducks are considered delicacies in the Middle East. In Egypt birds can be bought live from the market, where they are brought, cackling in crates, from the villages. On a visit there, a hostess who entertained me for dinner described how she had run after the ducks that had escaped as she carried them home.

Roast Chicken with Lemon and Garlic

Serves 4

* 1 chicken
* 2 tablespoons mild extra virgin olive oil
* juice of ½ lemon
* salt and pepper
* 2 garlic cloves, crushed

Rub the chicken with a mixture of olive oil, lemon juice, salt, pepper and garlic. Put it breast side down in a baking dish in a preheated 180°C (350°F, gas 4) oven.

Roast for 25 minutes per pound or until the chicken is well cooked and the breast is browned, turning it breast side up about midway.

Variation

* Rub the chicken with a mixture of 2 tablespoons of olive or sunflower oil, 1 teaspoon of ground cinnamon, ½ teaspoon of ground allspice, salt and pepper.

Skewered Chicken Pieces

Serves 4

* 4 chicken breasts
* 4 tablespoons olive oil
* 2–4 garlic cloves, crushed
* juice of ½ lemon
* salt and pepper

To garnish

* a bunch of flat-leaf parsley, chopped
* 1 lemon, peeled and cut into small dice
* 1 mild red onion, finely sliced
* 2 teaspoons sumac (optional)

Be careful not to overcook, as the chicken pieces quickly dry out. You may also use leg meat, which is juicier. The flavouring is Lebanese. Look at the variations for alternatives.

Cut the chicken into 2½ cm (1in) pieces. Mix the oil, garlic, lemon juice, salt and pepper and leave the chicken in this marinade for 30 minutes or longer.

Thread on to flat-bladed skewers and cook over a charcoal fire or under the grill for 6–10 minutes, turning the skewers over once, and brushing with the marinade.

Serve at once on a bed of parsley, diced lemon and sliced onion. Sprinkle, if you like, with sumac.

Variations

* For a Turkish marinade, liquidize in the food processor 1 onion with 4 tablespoons of olive oil, 1 teaspoon of ground cinnamon, salt and pepper.
* For a Moroccan flavour, use as a marinade ¼ teaspoon of ground ginger, 1 teaspoon of paprika, a good pinch of chilli powder and salt mixed with 4 tablespoons of olive oil. Serve with chopped coriander.
* For an Iranian version, turn the chicken pieces in 4 tablespoons of melted butter mixed with ¼ teaspoon of powdered saffron, the juice of ½ lemon and some salt.

Sautéed Chicken Breasts with Tomatoes

Serves 4

* 2 tablespoons butter
* 1 tablespoon sunflower oil
* salt
* 4 boned chicken breasts or chicken quarters
* 4 garlic cloves, crushed
* 500g (1lb) tomatoes
* 1–2 teaspoons sugar
* pepper

This is a quick and simple way with chicken.

Heat the butter with the oil in a frying pan. Put in the chicken breasts, season with salt, and brown them lightly on both sides.

Add the garlic, tomatoes and sugar and a little more salt and pepper and cook for 15 minutes (or 25 minutes if they are chicken quarters) or until the chicken is done but still juicy.

Chicken with Almonds and Honey

Serves 8

* 2 large onions, chopped
* 4 tablespoons sunflower oil
* 1 teaspoon ground ginger
* 1½ teaspoons ground cinnamon
* 2 chickens, cut into quarters
* salt and pepper
* ½ teaspoon powdered saffron
* juice of ½–1 lemon
* 250g (8oz) blanched almonds
* 1 tablespoon rose water
* 4–5 tablespoons honey

This chicken is quite magnificent if you like the way Moroccans mix savoury and sweet.

In a large saucepan, cook the onions with the oil until they soften. Stir in the ginger and cinnamon and put in the chicken pieces. Cover with water, add salt and pepper, saffron and lemon juice, and simmer, covered, for 30 minutes. Taste and adjust the seasonings (the sauce needs to be normally salty) and move the pieces so that the ones on top go to the bottom.

Lift out the chicken pieces and arrange them in a large, shallow baking dish. Remove the skins if you like and pour the sauce over the pieces.

Grind the almonds fairly coarsely in the food processor and mix with the rose water and honey. Spread this paste over the chicken pieces and bake in a 180°C (350°F, gas 4) oven for about 45 minutes.

Serve hot.

Chicken with Preserved Lemon and Green Olives

Serves 4

* 1 large chicken
* 3 tablespoons sunflower oil
* 1 onion, grated or very finely chopped
* 2 garlic cloves, crushed
* $1/4$ teaspoon saffron pistils, crushed with a spoon
* $1/2$ teaspoon ground ginger
* $1^1/2$ teaspoons ground cinnamon
* salt and pepper
* a good bunch of coriander, finely chopped
* a good bunch of flat-leaf parsley, finely chopped
* peel of 1–$1^1/2$ preserved lemons, cut into quarters
* 75g (3oz) green olives, soaked in 2 changes of water for 30 minutes

Preserved lemon (see page 84) gives the distinctive flavour to this famous Moroccan dish. The pulp is discarded and the skin alone is used.

Put the chicken into a large saucepan with all the ingredients except the preserved lemon and olives.

Half cover with water (about 300ml/$1/2$ pint) and simmer, covered, turning the chicken over a few times, and adding water if necessary, for about 45 minutes. Throw the lemon peel and drained rinsed olives into the sauce and cook for 20 minutes or until the chicken is so tender that the flesh pulls off the bone and the liquid is reduced.

Serve hot, with couscous if you like.

Chicken with Chickpeas

Serves 4

* 1 onion, finely chopped
* 2 tablespoons sunflower oil
* 1 teaspoon turmeric
* 1 large chicken
* 250g (8oz) chickpeas, soaked overnight
* juice of 1 lemon, or more to taste
* 2–4 garlic cloves, crushed
* black pepper or a pinch of cayenne
* salt

Lemon and turmeric give this dish, which my mother used to make, a yellow tinge and tangy flavour.

Fry the onion in the oil in a large saucepan until golden, then stir in the turmeric.

Put in the chicken and turn it until it is yellow all over. Add about 600ml (1 pint) of water, the drained chickpeas, lemon juice, garlic and pepper. Bring to the boil and simmer, covered, for 1 hour or longer, until the chicken is very tender, the chickpeas soft, yellow and lemony, and the liquid reduced, turning the chicken occasionally and adding salt when the chickpeas have softened.

Chicken with Tomatoes and Honey

Serves 4

* 4 chicken quarters
* 3 tablespoons sunflower oil
* 1 large onion, grated
* 1kg (2lb) tomatoes, peeled and cut into pieces
* salt and plenty of black pepper
* ½ teaspoon ground ginger
* 2 teaspoons ground cinnamon
* ½ teaspoon powdered saffron
* 2 tablespoons clear honey (Moroccans put up to 4 tablespoons)
* 100g (4oz) blanched almonds, coarsely chopped and toasted or fried in oil
* 2 tablespoons sesame seeds, toasted

In this Moroccan tagine *the chicken cooks in the juice of the tomatoes.*

Put all the ingredients except the honey, almonds and sesame seeds into a large pan and cook gently, covered, turning the pieces over occasionally, until the flesh is so tender it can be pulled off the bone easily.

Remove the chicken, and continue to cook the sauce over a medium heat until reduced to a thick sizzling cream. Stir as it begins to caramelize, and be careful that it does not stick or burn. Now stir in the honey, return the chicken pieces to the sauce and heat through.

Serve the chicken hot, covered with the sauce and sprinkled with the almonds and sesame seeds.

Chicken with Pasta

Serves 6

* 1 large onion, chopped
* 2 tablespoons sunflower oil
* 1 large chicken
* 4 cloves, sliced
* 2 teaspoons ground cinnamon
* 2 teaspoons ground cardamom
* ½ teaspoon ground ginger
* salt and pepper
* 400g (14oz) Italian *pastine graniamo*
* 2 tablespoons butter

A pasta which looks like large grains of rice, called lissan al asfour *(birds' tongues) in Arabic, is used in this dish. It cooks in the sauce from the chicken and acquires a delicate flavour and brown colour. You will find it in Middle Eastern as well as Italian stores.*

In a pan large enough to contain the chicken, fry the onion in the oil until soft.

Put in the chicken and pour in 1 litre (1¾ pints) of water (it will not cover the chicken entirely). Add the garlic, cinnamon, cardamom, ginger, salt and pepper. Simmer for 1 hour with the lid on, turning the chicken over once half-way through.

Take out the chicken, and when it is cool enough to handle remove the skin and bones.

Bring the sauce to the boil and throw in the pasta. Cook for 15 minutes or until tender, adding boiling water – about 250ml (9fl oz) – if necessary, and salt and pepper.

Stir in the butter and put the chicken pieces back into the pan on top of the pasta. Heat through before serving. The pasta becomes soft rather than al dente.

Variation
* Vermicelli, crushed into small pieces with your hands, can be used instead of the little *pastine*.

Roast Mediterranean Pigeons or Poussins with Dates

Serves 4

* 5cm (2in) fresh root ginger, grated or crushed in a garlic press to extract the juice
* 2 garlic cloves, crushed
* 4 tablespoons extra virgin olive oil
* juice of 1 lemon
* salt and pepper
* 2 tablespoons honey
* 4 young Mediterranean pigeons or small poussins
* 300g (10oz) dates, pitted
* 1 teaspoon ground cinnamon
* 50g (2oz) sesame seeds (optional)

The combination of chicken or meat with dates is very ancient in the Arab world. This recipe is inspired by a Moroccan one where the pigeons are stewed rather than roasted. Make this with young Mediterranean pigeons (which some butchers sell) or with poussins. I made it with baby partridge and it was delicious. Use dried dates of a soft moist variety.

Mix the ginger and garlic with the olive oil and the juice of $1/2$ a lemon. Add salt and pepper and 1 tablespoon of honey and beat well. Turn the birds in this marinade. Arrange on a baking dish breast side down. Roast in a preheated 220°C (425°F, gas 7) oven for about 15 minutes. Turn them over and roast for another 10 minutes or until they are done to your taste.

Put the dates in a pan and only just cover with water. Add cinnamon and the remaining honey and lemon and cook for 10 minutes until the dates are soft and have absorbed the flavours.

Serve the dates in the centre, the pigeons around, and sprinkle the sesame seeds all over.

Pigeons or Poussins Stuffed with Bulgur, Raisins and Pine Nuts

Serves 6

* 6 baby Mediterranean pigeons (*pigeonneaux*) or small poussins

For the marinade

* 1 large onion
* juice of 1 lemon
* 6 tablespoons sunflower or vegetable oil
* salt and pepper
* 1½ teaspoons ground cardamom
* 1½ teaspoons ground cinnamon
* ¾ teaspoon ground allspice

For the stuffing

* 1 litre (1¾ pints) stock (you may use 2 chicken stock cubes)
* 500g (1lb 2oz) coarse bulgur (cracked wheat)
* salt and pepper
* 1½ teaspoons ground cinnamon
* 100g (4oz) pine nuts
* 5 tablespoons butter or vegetable oil
* 100g (4oz) raisins or sultanas, soaked in water for 15 minutes

Stuffed pigeon is a delicacy of Egypt. Our tough gamy English pigeons are a different bird to the Mediterranean ones you need here. A few butchers sell them but small poussins will also do very well.

For the marinade, put the onion, cut into pieces, the lemon, oil, salt and pepper, cardamom, cinnamon and allspice into a blender or food processor and liquidize.

For the stuffing, bring the stock to the boil in a pan. Add the bulgur, salt, pepper and cinnamon and stir, then cook, covered, on a very low heat for about 15 minutes or until the liquid is absorbed and the grain is almost tender. Turn off the lid and leave, with the lid on, for 10 minutes more. Fry the pine nuts in 1 tablespoon of the butter or oil, stirring and turning them until lightly browned. Add the pine nuts, the drained raisins and the remaining butter or oil to the bulgur in the pan, and mix well.

Spoon some of the stuffing into each of the birds so that the cavity is three-quarters full, leaving room for the bulgur to expand, and secure the openings with toothpicks. Spread each bird with some of the marinade mixture and arrange in a baking dish, breast side down. Roast in a preheated 180°C (350°F, gas 4) oven for about 35 minutes, then turn over and roast for another 30 minutes or until golden brown and the juices no longer run pink when you cut into the thick part of a thigh.

At the same time reheat the remaining bulgur stuffing in a baking dish in the oven, covered with foil, for 20 minutes.

Pigeons or Poussins Stuffed with Couscous

Serves 4

* 4 pigeons or poussins
* 3 tablespoons butter or sunflower oil
* 1½ large onions, finely chopped or grated
* 2 garlic cloves, crushed
* 2 teaspoons ground cinnamon
* ¼ teaspoon ground ginger
* ½ teaspoon powdered saffron
* salt and plenty of pepper
* 2 tablespoons honey

For the stuffing

* 500g (1lb 2oz) couscous
* salt
* 1–2 tablespoons caster sugar
* 3 tablespoons sunflower oil
* 1 tablespoon ground cinnamon
* 2 tablespoons orange-blossom water
* 3 tablespoons raisins, soaked in warm water for 10 minutes
* 200g (7oz) blanched almonds, toasted and coarsely chopped
* 2 tablespoons butter

A few butchers sell the baby Mediterranean pigeonneaux. Otherwise get small poussins. This is a stunning party dish.

To prepare the stuffing, moisten the couscous with a little less than its volume of warm salted water – about 600ml (1 pint). Stir well so that it is evenly absorbed. After about 10 minutes, stir in the sugar, 2 tablespoons of the oil, the cinnamon and the orange-blossom water. Add the drained raisins. Fry the almonds in the remaining oil, coarsely chop them and stir them into the couscous.

Fill each poussin with about 3 tablespoons of stuffing. They should not be too tightly packed or the stuffing may burst out. Sew up the skin at both ends with cotton thread (or use tooth-picks to secure) and reserve the remaining stuffing.

In a wide and heavy saucepan put the butter or oil, the onions, garlic, cinnamon, ginger, saffron, salt and pepper. Add 300ml (10fl oz) of water and the stuffed poussins.

Simmer gently, covered, for about 30 minutes or until the birds are tender, adding more water if necessary and turning them over at least once, ending up breast side down, so that they are well impregnated with the sauce. Lift one out (to make a little room) and stir in the honey. Return the poussin to the pan and continue to cook until the flesh is at melting tenderness.

Heat the remaining stuffing in a baking dish, covered with foil, in a 200°C (400°F, gas 6) oven for about 20 minutes. Stir in the butter.

To serve, make a mound of the stuffing and place the birds on top.

Quails with Grapes

Serves 4

* 8 quails
* 3 tablespoons sunflower or
  vegetable oil
* 60g (2¹/₂oz) butter
* salt and pepper
* 8cm (3in) fresh root ginger or
  to taste, grated or crushed in a
  garlic press to extract the juice
* 3 garlic cloves, crushed
* 500g (1lb) seedless large white
  grapes, washed and drained

In Morocco, where this exciting dish is from, ground ginger is used, but with fresh ginger it is particularly delicious. I peel and cut the root into small pieces and press them through a garlic press. The juice and some soft bits are squeezed out.

Quails are often sold with some remaining feathers which need to be pulled out or burnt off.

In a large frying pan, heat 1 tablespoon of the oil with the butter. Put in the quails and sauté briskly over a medium heat for about 8 minutes, turning to brown them lightly all over, and adding salt, pepper and the ginger. Add the garlic and cook moments more until it begins to colour, then take off the heat.

Put the grapes with the remaining oil in a saucepan. Sprinkle with a little salt and cook, with the lid on, over a low heat for about 20 minutes or until the grapes are soft, stirring occasionally. Add them to the quails in the frying pan and cook for about 10 minutes or until the quails are done to your liking.

Serve hot.

Duck with Quince

Serves 4

* 4 duck legs
* 1 tablespoon olive oil
* salt and pepper
* 2 lemons
* 1 large quince weighing about
  750g (1½lb), or 2 smaller ones
* 1 teaspoon ground ginger
* 1 teaspoon ground cinnamon
* 2 tablespoons honey

There are many dishes of duck and chicken with quince in the Islamic world. This one has a sauce with the flavours of Morocco and the quince acquires a caramelized taste.

Rub the duck legs with oil and season with salt and pepper. Put them, skin side up, on a rack over a baking dish in a pre-heated 230°C (450°F, gas 8) oven for 30 minutes, until the skin is crisp and golden and the flesh still soft and juicy. If you do not have a rack, put them in a baking dish and pour out the fat as it is released. (If you don't do this the duck will fry in its own fat.) Reserve some of the fat.

Prepare a pan of boiling water acidulated with the juice of ½ a lemon. Wash and scrub the quince and cut into quarters. (This fruit is extremely hard so you will need a large strong knife.) You do not need to peel or core it. Simply remove any blackened ends. Put the quarters quickly (before they begin to go brown) into the boiling water and simmer until just tender (the time can vary between 10 and 30 minutes, depending on how ripe the fruit is). Be careful not to overcook. Drain, and when cool enough to handle, cut away the hard cores and cut each quarter into 3 slices (or 2 if the quinces are small). Set aside.

When the duck is almost ready, fry the quince slices in shallow oil until brown (this gives them a delicious caramelized taste), then lift them out of the pan.

Prepare the sauce: pour 2 tablespoons of the duck fat into a pan, stir in the ginger and cinnamon, the juice of the remaining 1½ lemons and the honey, add a few tablespoons of water and let it bubble up.

Serve the duck legs with the sauce poured over, accompanied by the quince.

Chicken Livers with Cinnamon and Allspice

Serves 4

* 500g (1lb) chicken livers
* 2 tablespoons sunflower or vegetable oil
* salt and pepper
* 1 teaspoon ground cinnamon
* ¼ teaspoon ground allspice
* 2 tablespoons chopped flat-leaf parsley

This is quick and simple. It can be served as a first course.

Sauté the chicken livers quickly in the oil over a medium heat, adding salt and pepper, cinnamon and allspice and turning the livers over, until they are brown but still pink and juicy inside.

Sprinkle with parsley and serve hot.

Meat Meat is the prestige food of the Middle East. With not enough humidity for cattle-raising, mutton and lamb are the traditional meats. But these days they are sometimes replaced by beef or veal, the recipes remaining unchanged. Many of the traditional combinations of meats with vegetables, pulses or fruit in stews are to be found in different countries. It is the flavourings and methods which vary and make the difference.

Meatballs with Sour Cherry Sauce

Serves 6–8

* 250g (8oz) dried pitted Californian sour cherries
* 750g (1½lb) lean lamb or veal, minced
* salt and pepper
* ½ teaspoon ground allspice
* 1 teaspoon ground cinnamon
* oil
* 1 large onion, chopped
* juice of 1 lemon

This is an old family recipe which originates in Syria. It is easy to make now that semi-dried pitted sour cherries from California are available in supermarkets.

Rinse the sour cherries and soak them in water to cover for 30 minutes.

Put the meat in a bowl. Add salt, pepper, allspice and cinnamon, and knead vigorously to achieve a soft, pasty texture. Roll into balls the size of fat marbles and fry briefly in shallow oil, turning them and shaking the pan until they change colour all over. You will have to do them in batches. Lift them out with a slotted spoon. They should be pink and underdone inside.

In a large saucepan, fry the onion in 2 tablespoons of oil till soft and golden. Add the cherries with their soaking water and the lemon juice and simmer for 10 minutes. Add the meatballs and cook gently for 5–10 minutes, turning them until they are cooked through and have absorbed the cherry juices.

Serve with rice or, as was usual in the old days, on opened-up miniature pitta breads, soft side up.

Meatballs with Spinach and Chickpeas

Serves 6

* 750g (1½lb) beef, lamb or veal, minced
* 1 onion, grated or finely chopped
* salt and black pepper
* sunflower or vegetable oil
* 500g (1lb) fresh spinach
* 1 tablespoon butter
* 420g (1lb) tin of chickpeas
* 2–4 garlic cloves, crushed
* 2 teaspoons ground coriander

This is very like dishes recorded in early medieval Arab cookery manuals.

Put the minced meat and onion into a bowl. Add salt and pepper, mix well, and work with your hands to a soft paste. Roll into little walnut-sized balls and fry briefly in batches in shallow oil, turning them until they are brown all over but still pink inside. Drain on kitchen paper.

Wash the spinach leaves thoroughly, removing any thick stems, and drain well. Put them into a large pan with the butter and no extra water, and cook over a low heat for a minute or so with the lid on, until the leaves crumple into a soft mass. Cut up the spinach roughly in the pan, using a pointed knife, add the drained chickpeas, season with salt and pepper and stir well. Put in the meatballs, stir, and cover the pan. In Egypt it was usual to cook for a further 30 minutes, adding a little water, until the meatballs were very soft. I like the meat to be still a little pink inside so I cook them for a few minutes only.

The particular refinement of this dish comes from a fried mixture called *taklia* which is added at the end. Fry the garlic in 2 tablespoons of the oil with the coriander until the mixture smells sweetly. Stir this in at the end of the cooking.

Serve with rice.

Variation

* A Turkish way of eating this is smothered in yoghurt mixed with crushed garlic and a little salt, pepper and dried crushed mint. The whole is decorated with a sprinkling of scarlet paprika. In this case, omit the *taklia*.

Meatballs with Aubergine Purée

Serves 6

* 4 aubergines (about 1kg/2lb)
* 750g (1³/₄lb) minced lamb or beef
* 2 eggs, lightly beaten
* 3 tablespoons dry white breadcrumbs
* ³/₄ teaspoon ground cumin
* ³/₄ teaspoon ground allspice
* salt and pepper
* sunflower or vegetable oil
* 1 large onion, chopped
* 2–3 garlic cloves, finely chopped
* 1 large beef tomato, about 250g (8oz), finely chopped

Roast, peel and mash the aubergines as described on page 000.

For the meatballs, put the minced meat, eggs and breadcrumbs in a bowl with the cumin, allspice, salt and pepper, and knead with your hands to a soft paste. Or blend in the food processor. Shape the mixture into small balls and fry in shallow oil over fairly gentle heat, turning them until they are coloured all over. Remove and drain on kitchen paper.

In another large frying pan, fry the onion in 3 tablespoons of oil until soft and golden. Add the garlic and stir until it begins to colour, then add the tomato, salt and pepper and cook for a few minutes until reduced. Add the mashed aubergines, season again with salt and pepper, and cook gently, stirring, for about 8 minutes until much of the liquid has disappeared. Drop in the meatballs and simmer for 5–10 minutes.

Serve hot with rice or bulgur (cracked wheat).

Right Quails with grapes
Overleaf Tagine of lamb with peas, preserved lemon and olives

Meatballs in Tomato Sauce with Eggs

Serves 6

For the meatballs

* 750g (1½lb) minced lamb or beef
* 1 onion, very finely chopped
* 3 tablespoons finely chopped flat-leaf parsley
* salt and pepper
* a pinch of chilli powder, to taste
* 1 teaspoon ground cinnamon
* ½ teaspoon ground ginger
* 1 teaspoon ground cumin
* sunflower oil for frying

For the tomato sauce

* 2 onions, chopped
* 2 tablespoons olive oil
* 2 garlic cloves, crushed
* 750g (1½lb) tomatoes, peeled and chopped
* 1–2 teaspoons sugar
* salt
* 1 small fresh chilli pepper, seeded and chopped (optional)
* 3 tablespoons chopped flat-leaf parsley
* 3 tablespoons chopped coriander
* 6 eggs

You will need a large shallow pan or pot that can go on the table. In Morocco the cooking is finished in a shallow earthenware tagine which goes on top of the fire. Serve with plenty of warm bread.

For the meatballs, mix all the ingredients together except the oil and knead into a soft paste. Roll into marble-sized balls and fry them very briefly in batches in shallow oil, shaking the pan to colour them all over. Lift out with a slotted spoon.

In a large shallow pot which you can bring to the table, prepare the sauce. Fry the onions in the oil till soft. Add the garlic, tomatoes, sugar, salt and chilli pepper, and simmer for 20 minutes until reduced. Add the parsley and coriander, put in the meatballs and cook for 5 minutes.

Break the eggs over the sauce and cook until the whites have set.

Previous page Kofta with tomato sauce and yoghurt
Left Artichokes, broad beans and almonds

Minced Lamb Kofta on Skewers

Serves 4

* 750g (1½lb) lamb from the shoulder, with fat
* salt and pepper
* a large bunch of flat-leaf parsley (about 100g/4oz weighed with stalks)
* 2 medium onions, grated or finely chopped

In restaurants they chop all the ingredients by hand then chop them together, but you can achieve good results with the blade of a food processor if you do each ingredient separately. For a moist juicy kofta you need a good amount of fat. Most of it will melt away in the heat of the grill. You will need skewers with a wide thick blade to hold the minced meat and prevent it from rolling around. If you find it difficult you can always make the meat into hamburgers.

Blend the meat to a soft paste in the food processor, adding salt and pepper. Put it into a bowl with the parsley and the onion, drained of its juices, and knead well with your hands until well blended.

Divide the meat into 8 balls and wrap each one around a skewer, pressing firmly so that it holds together in a long flat sausage shape. Place the skewers on an oiled grill over a fire or on a rack under the grill and cook for about 8 minutes, turning over once.

Serve with warmed pitta bread.

Accompaniments

* Slice 1 large onion thinly and sprinkle generously with salt. Leave for 30 minutes until the juices run out and it loses its strong flavour. Then rinse and drain and sprinkle with 1 tablespoon of sumac.
* Serve on a bed of chopped flat-leaf parsley and mint mixed with 1 thinly sliced onion and sprinkled with 1 tablespoon of sumac.
* Serve with chopped flat-leaf parsley and diced lemon (the lemon is peeled and cut into tiny cubes).
* 8 or more roasted cherry tomatoes.

* 4 long mild green peppers (you find them in Turkish stores), roasted until softened.
* In Turkey they serve *kofta kebab* on a bed of yoghurt beaten with a sprinkling of salt, pepper, chopped flat-leaf parsley and mint and topped with chopped tomatoes.

Variations
* Optional seasonings: 1 teaspoon of ground cinnamon, or 1 teaspoon of ground allspice, or 1 teaspoon of ground cumin and 1 teaspoon of ground coriander.
* Add ½ teaspoon of red pepper flakes or a pinch of chilli powder.
* Instead of grilling the meat on skewers you can make it into hamburgers and grill them or cook them in a pan filmed lightly with oil.

Kofta with Tomato Sauce and Yoghurt

Serves 4

* 1 thin pitta bread
* minced lamb kofta (see page 116)
* 600ml (1 pint) thick strained Greek yoghurt, at room temperature
* 1 teaspoon paprika
* 2–3 tablespoons pine nuts, toasted or not
* 1–2 tablespoons finely chopped flat-leaf parsley (optional) to garnish

For the tomato sauce

* 500g (1lb) tomatoes, peeled and chopped
* 4 tablespoons olive oil
* salt and pepper
* 1 teaspoon sugar

Yogurtlu kebab is a mainstay of Turkish kebab houses, where it is traditionally served in a dome-shaped copper dish. It is a multi-layered extravaganza. There is toasted pitta bread at the bottom, covered with a sauce made with fresh tomatoes; then yoghurt sprinkled with olive oil coloured with paprika and with a sprinkling of pine nuts, and finally grilled minced meat kofta on skewers. At home I find it easier to shape them into small burgers. The tomato sauce and burgers must be very hot when you assemble the dish. The yoghurt should be at room temperature.

Put the tomatoes in a pan with 1 tablespoon of oil, salt, pepper and the sugar until they soften.

Toast the pitta bread until it is crisp, then break it into small pieces.

Shape the minced lamb kofta into 12 or 16 small hamburgers. Cook them on the grill, turning them over once, until they are brown outside but still pink inside.

In each individual plate or bowl put a quarter of the toasted bread. Cover with a quarter of the tomato sauce and with a layer of yoghurt. Mix the paprika with the remaining oil and dribble over the yoghurt, then sprinkle with pine nuts. Arrange the meat burgers on top. If you like, garnish further with chopped parsley.

Minced Meat with Aubergines and Yoghurt

Serves 4–6

* 3 aubergines (about 750g/1¹/₂lb)
* 4 tablespoons sunflower or extra virgin olive oil
* 2 onions, chopped
* 500g (1lb) minced lamb or beef
* salt and pepper
* 50g (2oz) pine nuts
* 500g (1lb) thick strained Greek yoghurt
* 3 tablespoons tahina (sesame paste) (optional)
* 2 garlic cloves, crushed

This intriguing layered dish with a delicious combination of flavours is a speciality of the city of Hama in Syria and is called batoursh.

Cook the aubergines under the grill or roast them in the oven, then peel, chop and mash them to a purée (see page 13) and beat in 2 tablespoons of the oil.

In a large frying pan, fry the onions in the remaining oil till soft. Add the minced meat, salt and pepper and cook, crushing the meat and turning it over, for about 8 minutes until it changes colour. Add the pine nuts and cook for 5 minutes more. Leave aside and reheat just before serving.

Beat the yoghurt with the tahina, if using, and the garlic.

To serve, spread a layer of the aubergine purée (warm or at room temperature) at the bottom of a serving dish. Pour the yoghurt (at room temperature) on top and cover with the hot minced meat and pine nuts.

Tagine of Lamb with Peas, Preserved Lemon and Olives

Serves 6–8

* 1kg (2lb) lamb, trimmed of some of the excess fat and cut into cubes
* 2 tablespoons sunflower oil
* 1 onion, chopped
* salt and pepper
* 1 teaspoon ground ginger
* a good pinch of chilli powder or chilli flakes (optional)
* ¼ teaspoon powdered saffron
* 1kg (2lb) fresh peas (weight shelled)
* 2 tomatoes, peeled and chopped
* peel of 1 preserved lemon, cut into pieces (see page 84)
* 12 green olives

Some of our supermarkets sell fresh shelled peas which are young and sweet. If these are not available, use frozen petits pois.

Put the meat in a large pot with the oil, onion, salt and pepper, ginger, chilli powder or flakes, if using, and saffron. Cover with water and cook, covered, for 1–1½ hours until the meat is very tender, adding water to keep it covered in its sauce.

Add the peas, tomatoes, preserved lemon peel and olives and cook, uncovered, for a few minutes longer, until the peas are tender and the sauce reduced.

Serve hot with bread or couscous.

Lamb with Artichokes and Broad Beans

Serves 6–8

* 1kg (2lb) shoulder of lamb, cut into large pieces
* 2 onions, sliced
* 4 tablespoons butter or vegetable oil
* salt and pepper
* 1 teaspoon ground ginger
* ½ teaspoon powdered saffron
* 800g (1¾lb) (2 packets) frozen artichoke bottoms, defrosted
* 400g (14oz) (2 packets) frozen skinned broad beans, defrosted
* juice of ½–1 lemon
* a bunch of coriander, chopped
* peel of 1 preserved lemon (optional) (see page 84)

This Moroccan stew is easy to make with the frozen artichoke bottoms and skinned broad beans available in Middle Eastern stores.

Put the meat with the onions, butter or oil, salt, pepper, ginger and saffron in a pan and cook, turning the meat over, for about 5 minutes. Cover with water and simmer, covered, for 1½ hours, or until the meat is very tender, adding water if it becomes too dry. Remove the lid and reduce the sauce at the end.

Add the artichoke bottoms, broad beans and lemon juice and cook until the artichokes are tender.

Sprinkle with the coriander and, if you like, garnish with the preserved lemon peel, cut into pieces. Serve hot.

Note

If you want to use fresh artichokes, see page 133 for how to prepare artichoke hearts and bottoms.

Lamb with Chickpeas and Chestnuts

Serves 6

* 1 large onion, chopped
* 3 tablespoons sunflower or olive oil
* 500g (1½lb) shoulder of lamb, trimmed of some of the fat and cut into pieces
* 1 teaspoon ground cinnamon
* pepper
* 100g (4oz) chickpeas, soaked overnight
* salt
* 2 teaspoons sugar or to taste
* 2 tablespoons raisins
* 500g (1lb) chestnuts, or 400g (14oz) frozen or vacuum-packed peeled chestnuts
* 1 tablespoon honey (optional)

A Tunisian dish.

In a large saucepan, fry the onion in the oil till soft. Add the meat and turn to brown it all over. Add the cinnamon, pepper and the drained chickpeas and cover with water. Cook for 1 hour or until the chickpeas begin to soften.

Add salt, the sugar and the raisins and cook for 30 minutes or until the meat is very tender.

To shell the chestnuts, make a slit with a sharp pointed knife on the flat side and turn them under the grill until the skins are lightly browned and begin to separate from the nuts. Peel them while they are still hot. Add them to the stew, stir in the honey if you like, and cook for 15 minutes more.

Note

If using frozen chestnuts, defrost them thoroughly before adding them to the stew, and cook 10 minutes more. Vacuum-packed peeled chestnuts also go in towards the end. If you want to use tinned chickpeas, drain a 420g (14oz) tin and put them in at the same time as the chestnuts.

Meat and Okra Stew

Serves 6

* 750g (1¹/₂lb) young okra (called *bamia* in Egypt)
* 2 large onions, chopped
* 3 tablespoons sunflower or vegetable oil
* 2 garlic cloves, chopped
* 1 teaspoon ground coriander
* 750g (1¹/₂lb) beef, lamb or veal, cut into 3cm (1¹/₄in) cubes
* 500g (1lb) tomatoes, peeled and sliced
* 1–2 tablespoons tomato paste
* salt and pepper
* juice of 1 lemon

In Egypt, the okra is cooked at the same time as the meat to melting softness, but I prefer it not quite so soft and put it in later. You can please yourself.

Wash the okra and trim the stem ends.

In a large pan, fry the onions in the oil until soft and golden. Start on a low flame with the lid on, then remove the lid and turn up the heat to medium. Add the garlic and coriander and put in the meat. Turn the pieces until they change colour all over.

Add the tomatoes, cover with water and stir in the tomato paste. Season with salt and pepper, and stir well. Simmer over a low heat for 1 hour. Then stir in the okra, add water if necessary, and cook until the meat and okra are tender and the sauce reduced.

Add lemon juice and serve hot with rice.

Lamb Stew with Aubergine Cream Sauce

Serves 8

For the stew

* 1 large onion, cut in half then in slices
* 3 tablespoons sunflower or vegetable oil
* 750g (1½lb) lamb or beef, cut into 2cm (¾in) cubes
* 2 garlic cloves, chopped
* 750g (1½lb) tomatoes, peeled and chopped
* 1 teaspoon sugar, or to taste
* salt and pepper

For the aubergine cream

* 1½kg (3lb) aubergines
* 4 tablespoons butter
* 3 tablespoons flour
* ½ litre (18fl oz) hot milk
* salt and white pepper
* 75g (3oz) grated kaşar or Cheddar cheese

Hünkâr beğendi, *which means 'Sultan's delight', is the name of the aubergine sauce which is the star of this very elegant Turkish dish. It serves as a bed for a meat and tomato stew. Serve it with plain rice.*

For the lamb stew, fry the onion in the oil until soft. Add the meat and garlic and cook, turning the meat until lightly browned all over. Add the tomatoes, sugar, salt and pepper. Cover with water and simmer, with the lid on, for 1–1½ hours, until the meat is very tender, adding water if it becomes dry, and letting the sauce reduce at the end.

For the cream, prick the aubergines with a pointed knife so that they will not burst. Put them on a sheet of foil on an oven tray and roast them in the highest oven for about 30 minutes or until they are very soft and their skins black and blistered, turning them over at least once. Alternatively, you can turn them under the grill for about 15 minutes.

Peel them when cool enough to handle. Chop them in a colander to allow the juices to run out. Use a pointed knife then mash them with a fork.

Melt the butter in a large pan. Add the flour and stir over a very low heat for about 2 minutes until well blended. Add the milk gradually, beating vigorously all the time to avoid lumps forming, and taking the pan off the heat when you pour in the milk. Cook, stirring, until the mixture thickens and the taste of flour has disappeared.

Stir in the mashed aubergines, season to taste with salt and pepper, and cook for a few minutes longer. Stir in the cheese and let it melt in before serving.

Serve the meat on a bed of the cream sauce or arrange the meat in the centre of a serving dish and the sauce in a ring around it.

Tagine of Lamb with Apricots

Serves 6–8

* 2 large onions, chopped
* 2 tablespoons sunflower or extra virgin olive oil
* 1½ teaspoons ground cinnamon
* ¼ teaspoon powdered saffron
* 1 teaspoon ground cumin
* a good pinch of chilli powder, to taste
* 1kg (2lb) leg or shoulder of lamb, trimmed of some of the fat
* 2½cm (1in) fresh root ginger, cut into slices
* 3 garlic cloves, crushed
* salt and plenty of pepper
* 500g (1lb) dried apricots

Use sharp natural dried or semi-dried apricots – not a sweetened variety, for this North African dish.

Fry the onion gently in the oil until soft.

Stir in the spices – the cinnamon, saffron, cumin and chilli powder – and put in the meat. Turn the pieces so that they are covered in the spice mixture. Add the ginger, garlic, salt and pepper, and cover with about ½ litre (17fl oz) water. Simmer, covered, for 1½ hours, turning the meat over occasionally and adding water if necessary.

Add the apricots and cook for 30 minutes more, adding water if necessary.

Tagine of Lamb with Prunes

Serves 6

- 1kg (2lb) leg or shoulder of lamb, cubed and trimmed of some of the fat
- 3 tablespoons sunflower oil
- 1 teaspoon ground ginger
- $\frac{1}{4}$ teaspoon powdered saffron
- 2 teaspoons ground cinnamon
- salt and pepper
- 1 large onion, finely chopped or grated
- 2 garlic cloves, chopped
- 350g (12oz) California pitted prunes, soaked for 1 hour
- 1–3 tablespoons liquid honey (optional)

Optional garnishes

- 3 tablespoons lightly toasted sesame seeds
- 100g (4oz) lightly toasted blanched almonds, left whole or coarsely chopped

Tagine barragog is one of the most popular sweet fruit tagines of Morocco. The name derives from the clay pot with conical lid called a tagine in which stews are cooked slowly over a fire. It does not have to be as sweet as it is sometimes made in Morocco, where the honey is mitigated with large amounts of black pepper. Serve it with plain couscous. Restaurants in Paris accompany it with a bowl of boiled chickpeas and one of boiled raisins.

Put the meat in a pan with the oil, ginger, saffron, 1 teaspoon of cinnamon, salt, pepper, onion and garlic. Cover with water and simmer gently, covered, for $1\frac{1}{2}$–2 hours until the meat is very tender, adding water to keep it covered.

Add the prunes, the remaining cinnamon and the honey, if using (I leave it out). Stir well and simmer for 30 minutes longer until the sauce is reduced.

Garnish, if you like, with toasted sesame seeds and almonds.

Serve with couscous.

Lamb with Quince

Serves 6

* 1kg (2lb) shoulder of lamb, cut into large pieces
* 2 onions, sliced
* 4 tablespoons butter or vegetable oil
* salt and plenty of pepper
* 1 teaspoon ground ginger
* 1/2 teaspoon powdered saffron
* 1kg (2lb) quinces
* juice of 1/2 lemon, plus 1 optional lemon
* 1 teaspoon ground cinnamon
* 3–4 tablespoons honey

This is a Moroccan version of a dish you find in several Middle Eastern countries.

Put the meat with the onions, butter or oil, salt, pepper, ginger and saffron into a wide pan and cook, turning the meat over, for about 5 minutes. Cover with water and simmer, covered, over a low heat for 1 1/2 hours, or until the meat is very tender, adding water if it becomes too dry. Remove the lid at the end to reduce the sauce.

Wash and scrub the quinces. Have ready a pan of boiling water with the juice of 1/2 a lemon. Cut the quinces into quarters (you will need a big strong knife and plenty of force, as they are very hard), but do not peel them, and drop them at once into the acidulated boiling water (the lemon stops them going brown). Simmer for 10–30 minutes until tender. The time varies greatly and you must watch them as they can fall apart very quickly. They should not be too soft. Drain, and when cool enough to handle, cut out the cores.

Put them into the pan with the meat, flesh side up. Sprinkle with cinnamon and pour a little honey on each. Squeeze the extra lemon, if using, over the stew. Cook for 5 minutes, then turn the quince pieces over and cook a few minutes more.

Meat Pie with Mashed Potatoes

Serves 6–8

* 1.3kg (2³/₄lb) floury potatoes
* salt
* 100g (4oz) butter, cut into pieces
* 200ml (7fl oz) milk

For the filling

* 2 onions, chopped
* 4 tablespoons sunflower or vegetable oil
* 1kg (2lb) minced lamb or beef
* salt and pepper
* 1¹/₂ teaspoons ground cinnamon
* ¹/₂ teaspoon ground allspice
* 100g (4oz) pine nuts
* 3 tablespoons raisins (optional)

The Arab equivalent of shepherd's pie is gently spiced and with pine nuts.

Peel the potatoes and boil in salted water until done. Drain and return to the pan. Mash them and stir in the butter and milk. Season with salt and beat well.

For the filling, fry the onions in the oil till golden, stirring occasionally. With a large quantity of onions it is better to start on a very low heat with a lid on until they are soft, and then let them colour with the lid off. Add the minced meat, salt, pepper, cinnamon and allspice, and cook, crushing and turning the meat over, for about 10 minutes.

Heat the pine nuts in about ¹/₂ tablespoon of oil in a frying pan, shaking the pan to brown them lightly all over, then stir them into the meat mixture. If you like, stir in the raisins.

Spread the meat filling on the bottom of a baking dish and cover with a layer of the mashed potatoes. Press down to flatten the pie and bake in a preheated 200°C (400°F, gas 6) oven for 30 minutes, or until the top is lightly brown.

Roast Leg of Lamb with Meat, Rice and Nut Stuffing

Serves 6–8
* 1 large leg of lamb
* 4 garlic cloves, cut into slivers
* 2 tablespoons sunflower or vegetable oil
* salt and pepper

For the stuffing
* 500g (1lb) minced beef
* 4 tablespoons sunflower oil
* 250g (9oz) long-grain rice
* salt and pepper
* 2 teaspoons ground cinnamon
* ½ teaspoon ground allspice
* 450ml (16fl oz) meat or chicken stock (you can use 2 stock cubes)
* 50g (2oz) split almonds
* 50g (2oz) pistachios
* 50g (2oz) pine nuts

The grandest Arab meal is a whole stuffed baby lamb. A large leg of lamb accompanied by the traditional stuffing called hashwa – *cooked separately – is a representative of this ideal.*

Make slashes in the lamb with a sharp pointed knife and insert the pieces of garlic. Smear the meat with oil and rub all over with salt and pepper. Put the meat into a large oven dish or tray and roast in a preheated 200°C (400°F, gas 6) oven for 15–25 minutes per 500g (1lb), depending on how well cooked you like the meat.

Prepare the stuffing. In a large pan, fry the meat in 2 tablespoons of oil, turning it constantly and breaking up lumps, until it has changed colour and the moisture has disappeared. Add the rice and stir well for a few minutes. Then add salt, pepper, the cinnamon and the allspice. Pour in the boiling stock, mix well, and simmer, covered, for about 25 minutes or until the rice is tender, adding a little stock or water if it becomes too dry.

Fry the mixed nuts in the remaining oil until they just begin to colour and mix them into the rice before serving.

Variation
* Add to the stuffing 1 teaspoon of ground cardamom and a good pinch of ground cloves and grated nutmeg.

Vegetables

While meat is the prestige food of the Middle East, vegetables and grain are the everyday food. They are treated with special affection and imagination.

Vegetable dishes are served as side dishes or as a separate course before or after the main dish. You will find more of these in the appetizer section.

Artichokes, Broad Beans and Almonds

Serves 4

* 1 tablespoon flour
* 300ml (½ pint) water
* 2–3 teaspoons sugar
* juice of 1 lemon
* 3 sprigs of dill
* 1–2 garlic cloves, crushed or finely chopped
* ½ teaspoon salt
* 2–3 tablespoons mild extra virgin olive oil
* 400g (14oz) (1 packet) frozen artichoke bottoms, defrosted
* 200g (7oz) skinned broad beans, defrosted
* 50g (2oz) blanched almonds

You can find frozen artichoke bottoms from Egypt that are difficult to tell from fresh ones, and frozen skinned broad beans, in Middle Eastern stores. But if you want to use fresh ones, see page 133 for preparing artichoke bottoms, and skin your beans if they are not young and tender.

In a small bowl mix the flour to a smooth paste with a tablespoon or two of the water, and pour into a pan with the rest of the water. Add the sugar, lemon, dill, garlic and a little salt and bring to the boil, stirring vigorously so that the flour does not go lumpy. Simmer for about 10 minutes then beat in the oil.

Put in the artichoke bottoms, broad beans and almonds, add more water if necessary to cover them, and cook gently for 15–20 minutes or until the vegetables are tender and the sauce reduced.

Serve hot or cold as a first course. An attractive way is to spoon the broad beans and almonds into the artichoke cups.

Artichokes and Preserved Lemons with Honey and Spices

Serves 4–6

* 3 garlic cloves, crushed
* 3 tablespoons extra virgin olive oil
* 1/4–1/2 teaspoon ground ginger
* a pinch of turmeric
* juice of 1 lemon
* 1½–2 tablespoons liquid honey
* peel of 1½ preserved lemons, cut into strips
* 500g (1lb) artichoke bottoms (about 12 small ones), fresh or frozen and defrosted
* salt

The Moroccan flavours – preserved lemon and honey with garlic, turmeric and ginger – make this a sensational dish. I prefer it cold as a first course. I make it with the frozen Egyptian artichoke bottoms that I find in Middle Eastern stores. If you want to use fresh ones, see below for how to prepare them.

Heat the garlic in the oil for a few seconds only, stirring. Take the pan off the heat and add the ginger, turmeric, lemon juice and honey and the preserved lemons. Put in the artichoke bottoms and add about 1/4 litre (9fl oz) of water and some salt. Put the lid on and simmer for about 15 minutes or until the artichokes are tender, turning them over so that every part gets to cook in the liquid, and adding a little water if necessary. The sauce should be reduced at the end.

To prepare fresh artichoke hearts or bottoms

To prepare artichoke hearts remove the hard outer leaves, peel the stems and cut away the hard spiky ends. Remove the chokes. Cut the hearts in halves or quarters if they are large.

To prepare artichoke bottoms cut off the stems at the base, trim all the leaves and remove the chokes.

Place in acidulated water (with 2–3 tablespoons of vinegar or lemon juice) to keep them from blackening.

Spinach with Raisins and Pine Nuts

Serves 4

* 500g (1lb) spinach
* 1 medium onion, chopped
* 2 tablespoons extra virgin olive oil
* salt and pepper
* 2 tablespoons pine nuts, lightly toasted
* 2 tablespoons raisins, soaked in water for 15 minutes

Wash the spinach and remove only the stems that are thick and tough. Drain well. Put the leaves in a pan with the lid on. Cook over a low heat until they crumple in a soft mass (they steam in the water that clings to them).

In another pan, fry the onion in the oil until golden. Add the spinach, season with salt and pepper, and stir in the pine nuts and raisins. Cook, stirring, for a minute or two.

Spinach with Tomatoes and Almonds

Serves 4

* 500g (1lb) spinach
* 1 onion, coarsely chopped
* 2 tablespoons oil
* 2 tomatoes, peeled and chopped
* salt and pepper
* 60g (2oz) blanched almonds, toasted or fried

Wash the spinach and remove only the stems that are thick and tough. Put into a pan with the lid on and no extra water over a low heat. Cook for a few minutes only, until the leaves crumple in a soft mass. Drain.

Fry the onion in the oil until soft and golden. Add the tomatoes, salt and pepper and cook until reduced a little. Add the spinach and stir in the almonds.

Serve hot.

Spinach with Beans or Chickpeas

Serves 6
* 500g (1lb) spinach
* 2 tablespoons sunflower or olive oil
* 400g (14oz) tin of haricot beans or chickpeas
* salt and pepper

Throughout the Middle East spinach is partnered with beans or chickpeas.

Wash the spinach and remove the stems only if they are thick and tough. Drain and put in a pan with the oil. Cover with the lid and put over a low heat until the leaves crumple to a soft mass – they will do so very quickly. Add the drained beans or chickpeas, season with salt and pepper, mix very well and heat through. If there is too much liquid, reduce it a little.

Variations
* For an Egyptian flavour, in a small frying pan fry 3 chopped garlic cloves with $1^1/2$ teaspoons of ground coriander in 3 tablespoons of olive oil until the aroma rises, and stir into the spinach.
* Fry 1 large chopped onion in 3 tablespoons of olive oil. Add 2 peeled and chopped medium tomatoes and 1 teaspoon of sugar and cook until reduced, then stir in the cooked spinach and the beans or chickpeas.

Cauliflower with Olive Oil and Lemon Juice

Wash a cauliflower and boil in salted water until just tender. Drain and break into florets.

Heat 2 tablespoons of extra virgin olive oil in a pan with the juice of 1 lemon, and add salt and pepper. Turn the cauliflower in this over a low heat until heated through. It absorbs the oil and lemon. Some people like to add a little crushed garlic with the oil.

Turnips with Dates

Serves 2–4

* 500g (1lb) young white turnips, peeled and sliced
* 2 tablespoons butter
* salt and pepper
* 6 fresh dates, peeled, pitted and cut into small pieces

Boil the turnips in salted water until only just tender and drain.

Heat the butter in a frying pan and sauté the turnips until they begin to colour. Season with salt and pepper, add the dates and cook through, shaking the pan and stirring.

Pumpkin and Chickpeas

Serves 6

* 500g (1lb) orange pumpkin
* 1 large onion, cut in half and sliced
* 4 tablespoons olive oil
* 4 medium tomatoes, peeled and chopped
* 1–2 teaspoons sugar
* salt and pepper
* ½ teaspoon harissa (optional) (see page 171)
* 420g (1lb) tin of chickpeas, drained
* a bunch of flat-leaf parsley, chopped (optional)

This North African combination of vegetables, fresh and dried, is called tbikha. *All kinds of vegetables – peppers, carrots, turnips, cardoons, spinach – are cooked with chickpeas and dried beans. Good-quality tinned chickpeas will do. The dish can be made hot and peppery with harissa but it is very good without.*

Peel the pumpkin, remove any pips and fibrous bits and cut the flesh into pieces.

Fry the onions in the oil, stirring occasionally, until golden. Add tomatoes, sugar, salt and pepper, and harissa if using, and stir well. Add the chickpeas and pumpkin. Moisten with 4–5 tablespoons of water and simmer, with the lid on, for 20–30 minutes or until the pumpkin is tender, adding parsley towards the end. The pumpkin releases plenty of its own water, but if it becomes too dry, add a little more during the cooking.

Serve hot.

Variation
* Add 1 red pepper, cut into ribbons, to fry with the onions.

Sautéed Potatoes with Garlic, Chilli and Coriander

Serves 4

* 500g (1lb) new potatoes
* salt
* 3–4 tablespoons extra virgin olive oil
* 3–4 garlic cloves, chopped
* 1–2 fresh chillies, chopped, or a good pinch of chilli flakes
* a large bunch of coriander or flat-leaf parsley, chopped

This is batata harra – *garlicky, peppery potatoes.*

Boil the potatoes in salted water until tender, then peel and cut into slices or quarters. In a pan heat the oil. Add the garlic, chillies and potatoes, sprinkle with salt, and sauté, turning the potatoes over until crisp and golden. Add the coriander or parsley and stir.

Mashed Potatoes with Olive Oil and Parsley

Serves 4

* 750g (1½lb) floury potatoes
* salt
* 6 tablespoons extra virgin olive oil
* pepper
* 3 tablespoons capers, soaked in water (optional)
* 4 tablespoons chopped flat-leaf parsley or coriander

This is as good hot as it is cold. Sweet potatoes can be used in the same way. You must try the variations, which can be served cold as appetizers.

Peel the potatoes and boil in salted water until soft. Drain, keeping about 100ml (3½fl oz) of the cooking water.

Mash the potatoes and beat in the olive oil. Add salt and pepper to taste and enough of the cooking water to give a soft, slightly moist texture. Then stir in the capers, drained and squeezed, and the parsley.

Variations

* Fold in some chopped black or green olives – about 12.
* Add 50g (2oz) of coarsely chopped anchovy fillets.
* Add ¼–½ teaspoon of turmeric to the cooking water or ½ teaspoon of harissa at the end.
* Add ½ teaspoon of ground cumin, ½ teaspoon of paprika, 3 tablespoons of chopped coriander, and the juice of ½ a lemon.
* With sweet potatoes, add 1 teaspoon of ground ginger to the cooking water, then pinches of powdered saffron, ground cumin and chilli powder when you mash them. Use chopped coriander leaves instead of parsley and if you like add the chopped peel of ½ a preserved lemon.

Spicy Sweet Potatoes with Sultanas

Serves 6

* 1kg (2lb) sweet potatoes
* salt
* 75g (3oz) butter
* pepper
* ½ teaspoon ground ginger
* 1 teaspoon ground cinnamon
* 2 tablespoons raisins or sultanas, soaked in water for 15 minutes

Peel the sweet potatoes and cut them into pieces. Boil in salted water for 15–20 minutes until soft. Drain and mash with a fork. Add butter, salt and pepper, ginger and cinnamon, and beat well. Then add the drained raisins or sultanas.

Spicy Root Vegetables

Serves 6

* 1 celeriac
* 3 carrots
* 3 turnips
* 1 sweet potato
* 5 tablespoons sunflower or extra virgin olive oil
* ½ teaspoon turmeric
* 2 teaspoons caraway seeds
* salt and pepper
* a good pinch of chilli powder, to taste
* juice of ½ lemon

This is a Tunisian way with winter vegetables. It can be eaten hot or cold. If you want to eat it cold, use olive oil.

Peel and dice all the vegetables and put them in a pan with the rest of the ingredients.

Half cover with water and cook on a low heat with the lid on for 20 minutes, or until the vegetables are done, turning them over so that they are all in the water for some time. (They will also cook in the steam.)

Remove the lid, reduce the liquid to a sauce, and serve hot or cold.

Okra in Tomato Sauce

Serves 6

* 500g (1lb) okra, preferably young small ones
* 1 medium onion, cut in half and sliced
* 3 tablespoons sunflower or light olive oil
* 2 garlic cloves, chopped
* 500g (1lb) ripe tomatoes, peeled and chopped
* salt and pepper
* juice of 1 lemon (optional)
* 1–2 teaspoons sugar or to taste
* a small bunch of flat-leaf parsley or coriander, chopped

In Egypt, lamb stew with okra and tomatoes is a common everyday meal. The meatless dish can be eaten hot with rice or cold as an appetizer. Use olive oil and the lemon juice if it is to be eaten cold.

Trim the caps and rinse the okra. Fry the onion in the oil until soft and golden. Add the garlic and fry till the aroma rises. Now add the okra and sauté gently for about 5 minutes, turning over the pods.

Then add the tomatoes, salt, pepper, lemon juice and sugar and simmer for 15–20 minutes or until the okra are tender and the sauce is reduced. Stir in the parsley or coriander and cook for a minute more.

Variation

* Use 1–2 dried limes, cracked open with a hammer, or 2 teaspoons of dried ground limes instead of the lemon juice. You can buy them in Middle Eastern stores.

Green Beans in Tomato Sauce

Serves 6

* 1 onion, coarsely chopped
* 3 tablespoons mild extra virgin olive oil or sunflower oil
* 4 garlic cloves, finely chopped
* 500g (1lb) tomatoes, peeled and chopped
* 500g (1lb) French beans, topped and tailed
* salt and pepper
* 1 teaspoon sugar
* juice of ½ lemon (optional)

Use olive oil and add lemon juice if you want to eat this cold.

Fry the onions in the oil until soft and golden. Add the garlic, and when the aroma rises, add the tomatoes and French beans. Season with salt, pepper and the sugar, add water if necessary to cover the beans, and the lemon juice if using, and simmer for 15–20 minutes or until the beans are tender and the sauce reduced a little.

Borlotti Beans with Onions and Tomatoes in Olive Oil

Serves 6

* 250g (9oz) borlotti beans, soaked overnight
* 1 large onion, sliced
* 6 tablespoons extra virgin olive oil
* 3 garlic cloves, chopped
* 2 large tomatoes (about 500g/1lb), skinned and chopped
* 1 tablespoon tomato paste
* 1–2 teaspoons sugar
* a good pinch of chilli powder or dried chilli flakes
* a bunch of dill, chopped
* salt
* a bunch of parsley, chopped

Beans pilaki *(in olive oil), eaten at room temperature, are a Turkish staple. Mottled pink borlotti beans (they are called* barbunya, *which is also the name for red mullet) are a special treat. The Turkish ones obtainable here need to be picked over for foreign matter.*

Drain the beans and boil them in fresh unsalted water for 30 minutes.

Fry the onion in 2 tablespoons of the oil until soft and golden, stirring occasionally. Add the garlic and stir for a minute or so. Then add the tomatoes and cook gently until reduced to a pulp. Stir in the tomato paste, sugar and chilli powder or flakes. Put in the drained beans and cover with about 1/2 litre (17fl oz) of water. Cook, covered, for 1 hour or until the beans are tender (the time varies quite a bit), adding more water as it becomes dry. Add the dill and salt and the remaining oil, and cook for a few minutes more.

Stir in the parsley and leave to cool in the pan.

Right Tomatoes stuffed with minced meat, raisins and pine nuts; and stuffed artichoke bottoms with meat and pine nuts
Overleaf Couscous with poussins and almonds

Lentil Purée

Serves 4

* 1 onion, sliced
* 2 tablespoons oil
* 2–3 garlic cloves, crushed
* 250g (8oz) red lentils
* $^3/_4$ teaspoon ground cumin
* $^3/_4$ teaspoon ground coriander
* salt and pepper
* a pinch of chilli powder or dried chilli flakes (optional)

This is an Egyptian way with lentils.

Fry the onion in the oil until soft and golden. Stir in the garlic, and when the aroma rises, add the lentils. Cover with water, add the cumin and coriander, and stir well. Cook, covered, on a very low heat, adding salt and pepper and the chilli powder or flakes, if using, when the lentils disintegrate, and more water as required, being careful not to let the bottom burn.

Previous page **Sweet jewelled rice**
Left **Bulgur pilaf with tomatoes and aubergines**

Green Lentils in Tomato Sauce

Serves 4

* 2 garlic cloves, crushed
* 5 tablespoons extra virgin olive oil
* 3 medium tomatoes, peeled and chopped
* 125g (4½oz) large green or brown lentils
* salt and pepper
* a good bunch of flat-leaf parsley, finely chopped

This is good hot or cold, with plenty of raw olive oil.

Heat the garlic in 2 tablespoons of the oil for a moment or two, until the aroma rises. Add the tomatoes and cook for 3 minutes. Then add the lentils and about 350ml (12fl oz) of water. Stir and simmer, covered, over a low heat for 30–40 minutes until the lentils are tender, adding salt and pepper towards the end, and a little water if it becomes too dry.

Before serving, add the parsley and stir in 3 tablespoons of oil.

Peppers Stuffed with Rice

Serves 6

* 1 large onion, finely chopped
* 6 tablespoons extra virgin olive oil
* 250g (8oz) short-grain or risotto rice
* salt and pepper
* 1–2 teaspoons sugar
* 3 tablespoons pine nuts
* 3 tablespoons raisins
* 1 large tomato, peeled and chopped
* 1/2 teaspoon ground cinnamon
* 1/4 teaspoon ground allspice
* 2 teaspoons dried mint
* 3 tablespoons chopped dill or flat-leaf parsley
* juice of 1 lemon
* 6 medium green or red peppers

This is an old classic that has been adopted in all the lands that were once part of the Ottoman empire. It is meant to be eaten cold but is also good hot. Choose peppers that can stand on their base.

Fry the onion in 3 tablespoons of the oil until soft. Add the rice and stir until thoroughly coated and translucent. Pour in 450ml (16fl oz) of water and add salt, pepper and the sugar. Stir well and cook for 15 minutes or until the water has been absorbed but the rice is still a little underdone. Stir in the pine nuts, raisins and tomato, the cinnamon and allspice, mint and dill or parsley, lemon juice and the rest of the oil.

To stuff the peppers, cut a circle around each one at the stalk end and cut out a cap (with the stalk). Remove the cores and seeds with a spoon and fill with the rice mixture. Replace the caps. Arrange side by side in a shallow baking dish, pour about a finger of water at the bottom, and bake at 190°C (375°F, gas 5) for 45–55 minutes or until the peppers are tender. Be careful that they do not fall apart.

Serve at room temperature.

Tomatoes Stuffed with Herby Rice

Serves 4

* 1 medium onion, chopped
* 3 tablespoons extra virgin olive oil
* 1½ teaspoons tomato paste
* 125g (4½oz) round risotto or pudding rice
* 300ml (½ pint) water
* salt and pepper
* 1 tablespoon chopped mint
* 1 tablespoon chopped dill
* 2 tablespoons chopped parsley
* juice of ½–1 lemon or 1 tablespoon sumac
* ¼ teaspoon ground allspice
* 1 teaspoon ground cinnamon
* 4 large firm beef tomatoes or 10 small tomatoes

You can serve these hot or cold.

For the filling, fry the onion in 1 tablespoon of the oil until golden. Stir in the tomato paste and the rice. Add the water, salt and pepper, stir well, and simmer for 12 minutes or until the water is absorbed. Mix in the mint, dill and parsley, the lemon juice or sumac, allspice and cinnamon, and the remaining oil.

Cut a small circle around each tomato at the stalk end and cut out a cap. Remove the centre and seeds with a pointed teaspoon. Fill with the rice filling and replace the caps. Arrange in a shallow baking dish and bake in a preheated 180°C (350°F, gas 4) oven for 30 minutes, or until the tomatoes are soft, keeping watch so that they do not fall apart too quickly.

Tomatoes Stuffed with Minced Meat, Raisins and Pine Nuts

Serves 4

* 4 large beef tomatoes
* 1 onion, chopped
* 3 tablespoons sunflower oil
* 250g (8oz) lean minced lamb or beef
* salt and pepper
* 1 tablespoon raisins
* 2 tablespoons pine nuts or coarsely chopped walnuts
* 1/2 teaspoon ground cinnamon
* 1/2 teaspoon ground allspice
* 3 tablespoons finely chopped flat-leaf parsley

These are served hot.

Cut a circle around each tomato at the stalk end and cut out a cap. Remove the centre and seeds with a pointed teaspoon.

Fry the onion in oil until golden. Add the meat, salt and pepper. Turn the meat over and squash it with a fork until it changes colour. Stir in the raisins and pine nuts or walnuts and add the cinnamon, allspice and parsley.

Fill the tomatoes with this mixture and cover with their tops. Put them close to each other in a baking dish and bake in a preheated 180°C (350°F, gas 4) oven for about 30 minutes or until the tomatoes are soft, being careful that they do not fall apart.

Stuffed Artichoke Bottoms with Meat and Pine Nuts

Serves 4

* 1 onion, chopped
* 2 tablespoons sunflower oil
* 2 tablespoons pine nuts
* 300g (10oz) minced veal, lamb or beef
* 2 tablespoons finely chopped flat-leaf parsley
* salt and pepper
* ½ teaspoon ground cinnamon
* ¼ teaspoon ground allspice
* 1 small egg, lightly beaten
* 400g (14oz) (1 packet) frozen artichoke bottoms, defrosted
* juice of ½–1 lemon

Look for frozen artichoke bottoms – a flat cup variety produced in Egypt – in Middle Eastern stores.

Fry the onion in the oil until golden. Add the pine nuts and stir until lightly coloured.

Mix the meat, parsley, salt and pepper, cinnamon, allspice and egg, and knead to a soft paste with your hands. Then work in the onions and pine nuts.

Take lumps of the meat mixture and fill the artichoke bottoms, making little mounds. Place them in a shallow baking dish.

Mix the lemon juice with about 150ml (¼ pint) of water and pour into the dish. Cover with foil and bake in a preheated 180°C (350°F, gas 4) oven for 30–45 minutes until the meat is done.

Serve hot or cold.

Onion Rolls Stuffed with Meat in Tamarind Sauce

Serves 4–6

* 2 large mild onions
* 500g (1lb) lean minced lamb or beef
* salt and pepper
* 1 teaspoon ground cinnamon
* ½ teaspoon ground allspice
* 3 tablespoons finely chopped flat-leaf parsley
* 1½ tablespoons tamarind paste
* 1½ tablespoons sugar
* 3 tablespoons sunflower oil

Peel the onions and cut off the ends. With a sharp knife make a cut on one side of each, from top to bottom, through to the centre – and no further. Throw into a big pan of boiling water and boil for 10–15 minutes until they soften and begin to open so that each layer can be detached. Drain, and when cool enough to handle, separate each layer carefully.

For the filling, knead the minced meat with the salt, pepper, cinnamon, allspice and parsley. Put a small walnut-sized lump into each curved onion layer and roll up tightly. Line the bottom of a wide, shallow pan with discarded bits of onion (this is to protect the rolls). Pack the stuffed onion rolls tightly on top.

Melt the tamarind paste and 1 tablespoon of sugar in about 150ml (¼ pint) of boiling water, add the oil, and pour over the onions. Add more water to cover, if necessary. Place a plate on top to hold the onions and simmer, covered, on a very low heat, adding more water, as required, for about 45–60 minutes until they are very soft and the water is absorbed.

Now arrange the rolls in one layer on a flat, heatproof serving dish, sprinkle the top with the remaining sugar and caramelize under the grill. It gives them a warm wrinkly look.

They are best served hot but are also very good cold.

Rice, Bulgur and Couscous

Rice and bulgur are staples in Turkey and the Arab world. While bulgur is rural food, rice is a city dish. In my family in Egypt there was never a day without rice at the table. Couscous is the staple of North Africa.

Plain Rice

Serves 6
* 500g (1lb 2oz) basmati or long-grain rice
* salt
* 4 tablespoons butter or sunflower oil

Rice is the staple of the Arab and Ottoman worlds. Different varieties are used and every country has its own special ways of making it. Long-grain varieties, including the preferred basmati, are used for rice dishes. Short-grain or round rice is used only for stuffings and milk puddings and sometimes also in soups. It is traditional almost everywhere to soak it in a bowl of hot salted water for 30 minutes, but because of the way our rice here is processed, with some exceptions that is no longer an obligation. I am especially fond of basmati rice because of its wonderful aroma and capacity to stay separate. This rice needs to be washed. One way is to pour boiling water over it in a bowl, stir well, then rinse it in a sieve under cold running water.

The following method works well with all kinds of rice.

Bring plenty of salted water to the boil. Pour in the rice and cook over a high heat for about 12 minutes until the rice is still slightly undercooked. Then drain.

In the same pan, heat half the butter or oil. Pour in the rice, add the remaining butter or oil and a little salt and stir well. Cover with a tight-fitting lid and steam on a very low heat for 15–20 minutes.

Rice with Herbs

Serves 6

* 500g (1lb 2oz) basmati rice
* salt
* a huge bunch of mixed herbs including tarragon, chives, flat-leaf parsley, coriander and dill, finely chopped
* 6 spring onions, finely chopped
* 4–5 tablespoons butter or sunflower oil

An Iranian favourite.

Pour boiling water over the rice in a bowl, stir well, then rinse it in a sieve under cold running water. Bring plenty of salted water to the boil. Pour in the rice and boil for about 12 minutes until the rice is still slightly undercooked. Throw in the herbs and spring onions and drain at once. The herbs will cling to the rice.

In the same pan, heat half the butter or oil. Pour in the rice, add the remaining butter or oil and some salt. Stir well, cover with a tight-fitting lid and steam on a very low heat for 15–20 minutes.

Spiced Saffron Rice

Serves 6

* 500g (1lb 2oz) basmati or long-grain rice
* 900ml (1½ pints) stock (you may use a stock cube)
* 1 teaspoon cardamom seeds (Indian stores sell them out of the pod)
* 6 cloves
* 3 pieces of cinnamon bark
* ½ teaspoon powdered saffron
* salt and pepper
* 4–5 tablespoons butter or sunflower oil

This festive rice is beautiful and tasty.

If using basmati rice, pour boiling water over it in a bowl, stir well, then rinse it in a sieve under cold running water. American long-grain rice does not need rinsing.

In a pan, bring the stock to the boil with the cardamom seeds, cloves and cinnamon bark and simmer for 10 minutes. Add the saffron and a little salt and pepper and pour in the rice. Let it come to the boil again and stir well, then lower the heat to a minimum and cook on a low heat, with the lid on, for about 20 minutes, until little holes appear on the surface and the rice is tender.

Stir in the butter, cut into pieces, or the oil.

Serve the rice hot, in a mound, or press it into a mould and heat it through in the oven before turning it out.

Variations

* Sprinkle with a mixture of lightly toasted pine nuts and coarsely chopped almonds and pistachios, or throw these into the bottom of the mould before pressing in the rice.
* Add 3 tablespoons of raisins at the same time as the rice.
* Garnish if you like with 1 chopped onion fried until golden, or 3 tablespoons of raisins soaked in boiling water for a few minutes and 3 tablespoons of flaked or chopped almonds toasted under the grill or fried in 2 tablespoons of oil.

Rice with Vermicelli

Serves 4

* 50g (2oz) vermicelli, broken into 2.5cm (1in) pieces in your hand
* 2 tablespoons sunflower oil
* 250g (9oz) long-grain rice
* 600ml (1 pint) water
* salt
* 2 tablespoons butter

A popular everyday Arab rice.

Toast the vermicelli in a dry frying pan over the fire or in a tray under the grill until they are brown, stirring so that they brown evenly. Watch them, as they brown very quickly.

Heat the oil in a saucepan over medium heat, add the rice and stir until the grains are coated. Pour in the water, add the browned vermicelli and some salt, and stir well. Then simmer, covered, over a low heat for about 20 minutes or until the rice is tender and the water absorbed.

Stir in the butter and serve hot.

Variation

* Stir in a handful of boiled or tinned and drained chickpeas.

Rice with Raisins and Pine Nuts

Serves 6

* 1 large onion, chopped
* 3 tablespoons sunflower oil
* 400g (4oz) pine nuts, toasted
* 500g (1lb 2oz) basmati or
  long-grain rice
* 900ml (1½ pints) chicken stock
  (you may use a stock cube)
* ½ teaspoon ground allspice
* 1 teaspoon ground cinnamon
* salt and pepper
* 3 tablespoons raisins or
  currants
* 4–5 tablespoons butter or
  sunflower oil

A classic in all the countries that were part of the Ottoman empire.

If using basmati rice, pour boiling water over it in a bowl, stir well, then rinse it in a sieve under cold running water.

In a large pan, fry the onion in the oil until soft and golden. Add the pine nuts and stir until lightly coloured. Add the rice and stir over a moderate heat until well coated in oil.

Add the stock and stir in the allspice, cinnamon, salt and pepper and raisins or currants. Bring to the boil, then simmer, covered, over a low heat for 20 minutes or until the rice is tender and the water absorbed.

Stir in the butter or oil and serve hot.

Tomato Pilaf

Serves 4

* 250g (9oz) basmati or long-grain rice
* 1 onion, chopped
* 2 tablespoons sunflower oil
* 2 garlic cloves, crushed
* 2 teaspoons tomato paste
* 500g (1lb) ripe tomatoes, skinned and chopped
* salt and pepper
* 2 teaspoons sugar

If using basmati rice, pour boiling water over it in a bowl, stir well, then rinse it in a sieve under cold running water. Long-grain rice does not need rinsing.

Fry the onion in the oil until soft and golden. Add the garlic, and when the aroma rises, stir in the tomato paste and add the tomatoes. Season with salt, pepper and sugar and cook for 20 minutes.

Throw in the rice, and add enough water to cover the rice by about 2cm (3/4in). Bring to the boil and simmer, covered, over a low heat for about 20 minutes, until the rice is tender and the water absorbed, adding a little water if it becomes too dry.

Pumpkin Pilaf

Serves 4

* a slice of orange pumpkin (about 500g/1lb)
* 1 onion, chopped
* 2 tablespoons sunflower oil
* 300g (11oz) basmati rice
* 450ml (16fl oz) stock (you may use 1 chicken stock cube)
* 1 teaspoon cardamom seeds
* 1 teaspoon ground cinnamon
* salt and pepper
* 1 tablespoon raisins (optional)
* 3 tablespoons butter

Indian and Middle Eastern stores sell orange pumpkin, almost throughout the year, in slices with the seeds and stringy bits removed.

Pour boiling water over the rice in a bowl, stir well, then rinse it in a sieve under cold running water.

Peel the pumpkin and cut the flesh into $1^{1}/2$cm ($^{2}/3$in) cubes.

Fry the onion in the oil until golden. Add the rice and stir until the grains are covered in oil. Add the pumpkin and pour in the stock. Add the cardamom seeds and cinnamon, salt, pepper and raisins and stir well. Simmer, covered, on a low heat until the rice and pumpkin are tender.

Stir in the butter, and leave for a few minutes with the lid on before serving.

Sweet Jewelled Rice

Serves 6

* 500g (1lb 2oz) basmati rice
* 50g (2oz) semi-dried pitted sour cherries
* 50g (2oz) semi-dried cranberries
* 50g (2oz) barberries
* salt
* 75g (3oz) butter or 5 tablespoons sunflower oil
* ¼ teaspoon powdered saffron
* 4 tablespoons candied orange peel or coarse-cut orange marmalade, chopped (optional)
* 100g (4oz) split blanched almonds
* 50g (2oz) coarsely chopped or sliced pistachios

This Iranian rice is as sumptuous as you can get. Iranian and Middle Eastern stores sell barberries (sour berries called zeresk*), sugared orange peel and slivered almonds and pistachios. Some supermarkets sell semi-dried sour cherries and cranberries.*

Pour boiling water over the rice in a bowl, stir well, then rinse it in a sieve under cold running water. Soak the sour cherries, cranberries and barberries in water for 15 minutes.

Throw the rice into plenty of boiling salted water in a large pan and boil for about 10 minutes until partly cooked and still a little firm, then drain.

Heat half the butter or oil in the bottom of the pan and stir in the saffron. Pour the rice back in. Add the remaining butter or oil and the rest of the ingredients, also sprinkling with salt. Mix well so that the rice is evenly imbued with the saffron and the dried fruits and nuts are well mixed.

Put the lid on and steam on the lowest heat for about 20 minutes, until the rice is tender.

If you want to reheat it before serving, it is best to reheat it in a baking dish, covered with foil, as rice tends to burn at the bottom of the pan when it is dry.

Variation
* Instead of the sour cherries and cranberries use chopped dried apricots and chopped dates.

Sour Cherry Rice

Serves 6

* 500g (1lb 2oz) basmati rice
* 250g (8oz) semi-dried pitted
  sour cherries
* salt
* 100g (4oz) butter or
  5 tablespoons sunflower oil

A Persian rice. You can find semi-dried pitted sour cherries in a few supermarkets.

Pour boiling water over the rice in a bowl, stir well, then rinse it in a sieve under cold running water. Soak the sour cherries in water for 15 minutes.

Throw the rice into plenty of boiling salted water in a large pan and boil for about 10 minutes until partly cooked and still a little firm, then drain.

Heat half the butter or oil in the bottom of the pan. Pour the rice back in and add the drained cherries, sprinkling lightly with salt. Add the remaining butter or oil and stir. Steam, with the lid on, over a very low heat for about 20 minutes until the rice is done.

Bulgur Pilaf with Chickpeas

Serves 8

* 1 litre (1³/4 pints) stock (you may use 2 stock cubes)
* 500g (1lb 2oz) coarse bulgur
* 4 tablespoons butter or sunflower oil
* 400g (14oz) tin of chickpeas, drained
* salt and pepper

In many communities in the Arab and old Ottoman lands, cracked wheat or bulgur (pronounced burghul *in Arabic) – wheat that has been boiled then dried and ground – is the staple of the countryside and mountains. It is served, like rice, as an accompaniment to all kinds of dishes.*

Bring the stock to the boil. Pour in the bulgur and cook, covered, on a low heat for about 10 minutes or until the water is absorbed and the grain is tender.

Stir in the butter or oil, the chickpeas, salt and pepper, and heat through.

Variation

* Garnish with 1 large sliced onion fried in oil until caramelized and brown.

Bulgur Pilaf with Raisins and Pine Nuts

Serves 6–8

* 1 litre (1³/₄ pints) chicken stock (you may use a stock cube) or water
* 500g (1lb 2oz) coarse bulgur
* salt and pepper
* 100g (4oz) pine nuts
* 75g (3oz) butter or 4 tablespoons sunflower oil
* 50g (2oz) raisins or sultanas, soaked in water for 30 minutes

I often make this popular and versatile wheat dish as an alternative to rice.

Bring the stock or water to the boil in a pan. Add the bulgur, salt and pepper and stir, then cook, covered, on a very low heat for about 15 minutes or until the liquid is absorbed and the grain tender. Turn off the heat and leave, covered, for 10 minutes or until the grain is plump and tender.

Fry the pine nuts in a tablespoon of the butter or oil, shaking the pan until golden. Stir them into the bulgur with the remaining butter or oil and the drained raisins or sultanas and heat through.

Bulgur Pilaf with Tomatoes and Aubergines

Serves 6–8

* 1 large onion, chopped
* sunflower or olive oil
* 500g (1lb 2oz) bulgur
* 500g (1lb) tomatoes, peeled and chopped
* 2 teaspoons tomato paste
* 2 teaspoons sugar
* salt and pepper
* 1 teaspoon ground allspice
* 350ml (12fl oz) water
* 2 medium aubergines, cut into 2¹⁄₂cm (1in) cubes

This can be eaten hot or cold.

Fry the onion in 4 tablespoons of oil until golden. Add the bulgur and stir well. Add the tomatoes, tomato paste, sugar, salt, pepper and allspice and the water. Stir and cook, covered, over a very low heat for 15 minutes, adding a little more water if too dry, or letting it evaporate uncovered if too wet. Leave to rest, covered, for 10 minutes or until the grain is plump and tender.

Fry the aubergines in shallow oil until lightly browned and soft inside. Drain on kitchen paper. Mix gently into the bulgur.

Couscous

Couscous – pronounced seksou *in the Berber lands where it originates – is hard wheat which has been ground to various degrees of fineness, then moistened and coated with fine flour before it is cooked by lengthy steaming. The name also refers to the whole dish or set of dishes – soupy stew with meat and vegetables or a* tagine *and side dishes – which are based on the grain.*

The commercial varieties of couscous we get here are precooked and instant. You do not need to steam it in the traditional way. Once the grain has absorbed an equal volume of water, all you need to do is heat it through.

Making couscous

For 6 people, put 500g (1lb 2oz) of medium-ground couscous in a bowl. Add 600ml (1 pint) of warm salted walter (with ½–1 teaspoon of salt) gradually, stirring so that it gets absorbed evenly. After about 10 minutes, when the grain has become a little plump and tender, add 3 tablespoons of sunflower oil and rub the grain between your hands to air it and break up any lumps.

Heat it through by steaming in the top part of a couscoussière if you like the idea (it is ready as soon as you can see the steam passing through the grain), or more simply in the oven, covered with foil. A small quantity for 2 or 3 can be heated in a saucepan, stirring so as not to burn the bottom, or in the microwave. Before serving, break up any lumps very thoroughly and work in 2 tablespoons of butter or sunflower oil.

I usually make it for a large number of people straight into a huge clay dish which goes into the oven then on the table.

Variations

* For saffron couscous add $^1/_4$–$^1/_2$ teaspoon of powdered saffron to the water before moistening the couscous.
* Serve the grain mixed with boiled chickpeas and raisins.

Garnishes

* Sprinkle the grain with ground cinnamon and icing sugar and whole or chopped toasted blanched almonds, making a design with lines fanning down like rays from the top.
* Cover with walnut halves and raisins or sultanas.

Side dishes

* For caramelized onions cook, covered, 1kg (2lb) of sliced onions in about 4 tablespoons of sunflower oil over a very low heat, stirring occasionally, for about 20 minutes or until very soft. Then continue to cook, uncovered, and stirring often, until they are really very brown. Stir in 2 tablespoons of sugar and 1 teaspoon of ground cinnamon and cook for a few minutes more.
* Simmer 250g (8oz) of raisins in water to cover for about 10 minutes, until soft.
* Soak 250g (8oz) of chickpeas for at least 1 hour, then drain and simmer in fresh water for 1 hour or until very tender, adding salt when they begin to soften. Serve them hot in a bowl in their cooking water.

Couscous with Seven Vegetables

Serves 10

For the grain

* 1kg (2¼lb) couscous
* 1.2 litres (2 pints) warm salted water (with 1–2 teaspoons salt)
* 3 tablespoons sunflower oil
* 4 tablespoons butter or more oil

For the stew

* 1kg (2lb) lean lamb, cubed, or 500g (1lb) lamb and 1 small chicken, or 2 small chickens
* 2 onions, chopped
* 3 tomatoes, quartered
* 3 tablespoons sunflower oil
* salt and pepper
* ½ teaspoon powdered saffron or saffron pistils
* 4 carrots, cut lengthwise or into thick pieces
* 3 turnips, quartered
* ½ white cabbage, cut into chunks
* 3 courgettes, cut into big pieces
* 200g (7oz) fresh shelled or frozen broad beans
* 5 artichoke hearts or frozen artichoke bottoms (from Middle Eastern stores)
* 2 fennel bulbs, quartered
* 250g (8oz) slice of orange pumpkin, cut into pieces

Here is a classic Moroccan couscous around which you can improvise. It can be made with lamb or with chicken or with a mix of the two. In local lore, the number seven has mystic qualities. It brings good luck. Choose seven vegetables out of those listed – onions and tomatoes do not count as vegetables but as flavourings, so choose seven others. It is a long list of ingredients but the making of the dish is simple – a matter of throwing things in a pot. The hot peppery sauce that accompanies is more Tunisian and Algerian.

Prepare the couscous as described on page 168 in **Making couscous**, using twice the quantity.

Put the meat or chicken or both into a large pan with the onions and tomatoes. Cover with plenty of water, add the oil, salt, pepper and saffron, and simmer, covered, for 1 hour. Add the carrots and turnips and cook for 30 minutes more or until the meats are very tender.

Put in the remaining ingredients except the harissa, and add more water – you need to make plenty of broth. Cook for a further 30 minutes, adding more salt and pepper.

Make a hot peppery sauce to accompany. Take 3 ladlefuls of broth from the stew and stir in the harissa or paprika and chilli powder – enough to make it very strong and fiery.

To serve, pile the couscous on to a large dish. Add butter and work it into the grain as it melts. Shape it into a mound with a pit at the top. Arrange the meat at the top and the vegetables down the sides. Serve the broth in a separate bowl. Pass the broth and the hot, peppery sauce round for everyone to help themselves.

* 2 medium aubergines, cut into pieces
* 2 green peppers, cut into ribbons
* a large bunch of coriander, finely chopped
* 2 teaspoons harissa (see below, or use a bought variety), or 2 tablespoons paprika and $1/2$ teaspoon chilli powder or more to taste

Alternatively, serve the couscous separately and the meat and vegetables with the broth.

Variations
* 75g (3oz) of chickpeas, soaked overnight, may be added at the start (in which case do not add salt until they have softened), and 75g (3oz) of raisins or pitted dates may be added towards the end of cooking.
* $1/2$ teaspoon of ground ginger, 1 teaspoon of ground cinnamon and 1 teaspoon of ground coriander are other possible flavourings.
* Algerians add runner beans and peas.

Harissa

This chilli paste goes into many North African – especially Tunisian – dishes. It keeps very well for many weeks in the refrigerator, if covered with olive oil. A ready-made paste can be bought here.

* 60g (2oz) dried hot red chilli peppers (stems and seeds removed)
* 4 garlic cloves, peeled
* 1 teaspoon ground caraway
* 1 teaspoon ground coriander
* $1/2$ teaspoon salt
* extra virgin olive oil

Soak the chilli peppers in water for 30 minutes until soft, then drain. Pound them with the garlic, spices and a little salt, using a pestle and mortar, or blend in a food processor, adding just enough oil, by the tablespoon, to make a soft paste. Press into a jar and cover with oil.

Couscous with Poussins and Almonds

Serves 6

* 6 small poussins or 3 large ones
* 3 tablespoons butter or sunflower oil
* 500g (1lb) onions, chopped
* 500g (1lb) baby (pickling) onions, peeled
* salt and pepper
* 1/2–1 teaspoon saffron threads
* 1 teaspoon ground ginger
* 300g (11oz) almonds
* 100g (4oz) raisins (optional)
* a large bunch of coriander, chopped
* 1 teaspoon harissa (see page 171, or use a bought variety) or to taste, or 1 teaspoon paprika and 1/3 teaspoon cayenne (optional)

For the grain

* 500g (1lb 2oz) couscous
* 600ml (1 pint) warm salted water (with 1/2–1 teaspoon salt)
* 3 tablespoons sunflower or vegetable oil
* 2 tablespoons butter or extra oil

In Morocco, where they often make it with Mediterranean pigeons, they do not serve this elegant couscous with the peppery sauce harissa. But in Tunisia they do.

Put the poussins in a large saucepan with the butter or oil and the onions (an easy way to peel the pickling ones is to blanch them first in water, which loosens their skins).

Cover with about 2 litres (3 1/2 pints) of water. Add salt, pepper, the saffron, ginger, almonds and raisins, and cook, covered, for about 45 minutes, turning the poussins over. Add the coriander.

At the same time, put the couscous into an oven dish and add the salted water gradually, stirring so that it gets absorbed evenly. After about 10 minutes, when the grain has become plump and tender, add the oil and rub the grain between your hands to air it and break up any lumps. Cover with foil and heat through in a 200°C (400°F, gas 6) oven for about 20 minutes or until very hot.

Before serving, break up any lumps very thoroughly and work in 2 tablespoons of butter or sunflower oil. Shape into a mound and arrange the poussins on top (large ones cut in half). Serve the soup separately.

Variation

If you like, make a hot sauce to pass around for people to help themselves if they want to: pour 2 ladlefuls of the stock into a bowl and mix in some harissa or a mixture of paprika and cayenne.

Couscous with Peas

Serves 4

* 250g (8oz) couscous
* 300ml (½ pint) warm salted water (with ½–1 teaspoon salt)
* 1 tablespoon sunflower oil
* 250–500g (8oz–1lb) frozen petits pois
* 3 tablespoons butter or more

This is one of the very few traditional couscous dishes without meat. Another is with broad beans. As there is no sauce, they need plenty of butter. In the summer, tiny young fresh peas are sold podded in packets in some supermarkets. Otherwise frozen petits pois will do perfectly well.

Put the couscous in a bowl and add the salted water gradually, stirring so that it gets absorbed evenly. After about 15 minutes, when the grain has become plump and almost tender, add the oil and rub the grain between your hands to air it and break up any lumps.

Heat the couscous through in a pan, covered with a lid so that it steams. As it is a small quantity it is all right to do it in a pan, but you must be careful not to let it burn. Add a drop of water if necessary.

Cook the peas in salted water for minutes only until they are just tender.

Before serving, break up any lumps in the couscous and stir in the butter and the peas.

Desserts and Pastries

A Middle Eastern meal always ends with fruit. Puddings and pastries are for special occasions and for different times of the day when they are served with coffee or tea. For a dinner party offer an exciting selection of fruit such as figs, grapes, apricots, dates, cherries, Cape gooseberries, plums, nectarines and tangerines. Cut up into slices fruits such as melon, watermelon, mango, guava, pawpaw and oranges and arrange them on a platter. With coffee, offer dried fruit and nuts.

Oranges in Orange Syrup

Serves 4

* 6 oranges
* 100g (4oz) sugar
* 450ml (16fl oz) freshly squeezed orange juice
* 1 tablespoon orange-blossom water

The orange zest and the orange-blossom water give the syrup a special fragrance.

Grate the zest of 2 of the oranges, and put it into a pan with the sugar and orange juice. Bring to the boil and stir until the sugar has dissolved, then add the orange-blossom water.

Peel the oranges so that no pith remains. Cut them into thick slices then cut each slice into 4 pieces. Put them in a serving bowl and pour the orange syrup on top.

Serve cold.

Rose-scented Fruit Salad

Peel where necessary and cut up a variety of fruit such as melon, mango, bananas, oranges, apples, pears, apricots, nectarines, strawberries, seedless grapes, kiwis, cherries, and pineapple.

Sprinkle with a mixture of sugar, lemon juice and rose water. To serve 6 you may like 4 tablespoons of sugar, the juice of 1 lemon and 1–1¹/2 tablespoons of rose water. Leave to macerate for at least an hour before serving, turning over the fruit a few times.

Apricot Cream

Serves 6

* 500g (1lb) dried natural unsweetened apricots
* 750ml (1¼ pints) water
* 1 tablespoon orange-blossom water or rose water, or to taste
* juice of ½ lemon
* 1–2 tablespoons sugar, or to taste
* 100g (4oz) coarsely chopped pistachios or almonds
* 250ml (8fl oz) thick double cream or yoghurt, to serve

In Egypt, during the month of Ramadan, the daily fast is broken with a cream made from sheets of dried pressed apricots (amar eldin), soaked, then boiled in water. The sheets available these days do not have the pure taste they once had – perhaps due to preservatives. It is better to use natural dried apricots. Adding pistachios or almonds and thick cream are optional embellishments.

Soak the apricots overnight in the water. Put them through the blender or food processor, with enough of their soaking water to give a thick purée, adding orange-blossom or rose water, lemon juice and sugar to taste. Stir in half the pistachios or almonds.

Serve chilled, sprinkled with the remaining pistachios or almonds, accompanied by double cream or yoghurt.

Right **Almond 'snake'**
Overleaf **Oranges in orange syrup**

Macerated Apricots and Nuts

Serves 6

- 500g (1lb) dried apricots
- 1 litre (1¼ pints) water
- 50g (2oz) blanched almonds
- 25g (1oz) pine nuts
- 25g (1oz) pistachios, coarsely chopped
- 1 tablespoon rose water
- 2 tablespoons sugar (optional)

This delicately fragrant sweet is an old Syrian speciality of Ramadan, the Muslim month of fast. It keeps very well for days, even weeks, covered with clingfilm in the refrigerator.

Soak the apricots in the water overnight.

Drain, reserving the soaking water. Take a dozen of the apricots and blend to a light purée with the water in the food processor. Add to the rest of the apricots in a serving bowl and stir in the rest of the ingredients.

Serve chilled.

Previous page Almond fingers; ma'amoul
Left Quince dessert

Baked Apricots Stuffed with Almond Paste

Serves 6

* 13 large apricots
* 200g (7oz) blanched almonds
* 100g (4oz) caster sugar
* 3 tablespoons rose water

The special appeal of this dish is the contrast between the sharpness of the apricots and the sweetness of the almond paste.

Cut around one side of the apricots and remove the stones.

Blend the almonds, sugar and rose water to a soft paste in the food processor. Take lumps the size of a small walnut and roll them into balls. Push them into the apricot slits and press the apricots to squeeze the filling gently.

Arrange the stuffed fruits in a heatproof dish and bake in a preheated 180°C (350°F, gas 4) oven for about 20 minutes or until they have softened a little.

Serve hot or cold.

Prunes Stuffed with Walnuts in Orange Juice

Serves 6-8

* 500g (1lb) pitted prunes (the moist Californian or French types)
* 150g (5oz) walnut halves
* 400ml (14fl oz) freshly squeezed orange juice

Optional topping

* 300ml (½ pint) double cream, to serve
* 2 tablespoons sugar
* 1 tablespoon rose or orange-blossom water

Stuffing prunes takes time, but you can watch the television or listen to music while you do it. I prefer it without the cream topping.

Make the hole in the prunes a little wider with your finger and stuff each with half a walnut. Put them in a pan, cover with orange juice, and simmer over a low heat for 20–30 minutes or until they are soft, adding a little water if they become too dry. Serve chilled.

For the optional topping, whip the cream until it thickens and add the sugar and rose or orange-blossom water. Pour all over the prunes and chill together before serving, or, better still, pass round for everyone to help themselves.

Quince Dessert

Serves 4

* 2 large quinces (about 1kg/2lb)
* juice of ½ lemon
* 100g (4oz) sugar
* 150ml (¼ pint) clotted cream or thick double cream

You will find quinces in Middle Eastern grocers from October until February. One can weigh as much as 500g (1lb) and will do for 2 or 4 people.

Wash the quinces and scrub to remove the light down that covers their skin in patches. Cut them in half through the core but do not peel them. The fruit is extremely hard so you will need a strong knife and a lot of strength. You do not need to core them, and the pips are important as they produce a red jelly. Cook the quinces as soon as they are cut, as the flesh discolours quickly.

Have ready a pan of boiling water – about 600ml (1 pint) – with the lemon juice and sugar. Put in the fruit, cut side down, and simmer until it is tender and the syrup turns into a reddish jelly. The time varies greatly. The fruit can take from 20–60 minutes to be tender and the syrup can take more than an hour to turn into a reddish jelly. You have to watch the fruit so that it does not fall apart. If it becomes tender too quickly, lift it out, reduce the syrup by simmering, then return the fruit to the pan and cook until the syrup becomes reddish and thick. The thickened syrup has a hardening effect and prevents the fruit from falling apart. Arrange the quince halves, cut side up, on a serving dish and pour the syrup on top. It will turn into a jelly as it cools.

Serve chilled or at room temperature, with dollops of clotted cream or whipped double cream.

Note

* Cut the fruit into quarters if you find the portions too big.

Polenta Fritters

Serves 8
* 1 litre (1³/₄ pints) milk
* 250g (9oz) sugar
* a few drops of vanilla essence
* The grated rind of one lemon
* 250g (9oz) pre-cooked maize meal (polenta)
* 75g (3oz) butter, cut into pieces
* 5 eggs, lightly beaten
* 100g (4oz) currants or raisins
* flour
* sunflower or vegetable oil for deep-frying
* icing sugar to sprinkle on

This is the Algerian polenta annabi – soft and creamy inside. They are eaten hot, but you can prepare them in advance and reheat them.

In a saucepan, bring the milk to the boil with the sugar, the vanilla essence and grated lemon rind. Stir in the maize meal and keep stirring with a wooden spoon for 5–10 minutes.

Take off the heat, add the butter and the eggs, and beat vigorously with the spoon until they are amalgamated with the polenta into a soft creamy mass. Add the currants and raisins and mix well. Then pour into a wide, oiled dish and let it cool.

When the polenta has firmed, take lumps the size of a small tangerine and pat them into a round, not too flat cakes. Put some flour on a plate and turn the polenta cakes in this to cover them with flour.

Deep-fry in batches in hot oil until golden, turning them over once.

Serve hot, dusted with a little icing sugar.

Variation
* For a polenta cake, pour the polenta mixture into a 28–30cm (11–12in) oiled oven dish or tart pan and bake in a 180°C (350°F, gas 4) oven for 25 minutes, then put under the grill until golden. Serve cold, dusted with icing sugar. Cut into wedges.

Yoghurt with Honey

* 3cm (1¼in) fresh root ginger (optional)
* 300ml (½ pint) thick strained Greek yoghurt
* 1½ tablespoons liquid Greek honey, or more to taste

Peel and grate the ginger or, better still, cut it into pieces and press them in a garlic press to extract the juice over the yoghurt. Add the honey and beat well together.

Variations
* Yoghurt with rose-petal jam, which you will find in Middle Eastern stores, is a simple and delicious dessert.
* Fruit preserves such as quince, apricot or sour cherry may be used instead of honey.

Almond Cream

Serves 6

* 100g (4oz) blanched almonds
* 1 litre (1³/₄ pints) milk
* 2 tablespoons cornflour
* 2 tablespoons ground rice
* 100g (4oz) sugar
* a few drops of almond essence
* 2 tablespoons finely chopped pistachios, to garnish

Milk puddings are a speciality of the Middle East. This Turkish one with almonds, called keşkül, *is my favourite.*

Grind the almonds in the food processor (the texture is better if you do not use commercially ground ones).

Bring the milk to the boil and take off the heat.

In a small bowl, mix the cornflour and ground rice to a paste with 4–5 tablespoons of water, making sure there are no lumps. Pour this into the milk, stirring vigorously with a wooden spoon, and cook, stirring constantly, and always in the same direction, to avoid lumps forming, for about 15 minutes or until the mixture begins to thicken.

Add the sugar and almonds and continue to cook on the lowest possible heat, stirring occasionally, for 20 minutes or until the consistency is that of a thick pudding. Always stir in the same direction and do not scrape the bottom of the pan as you stir, as the bottom tends to stick and burn a little and you do not want to scrape up any burnt bits. Stir in the almond essence and pour into a serving bowl or individual bowls. Let the cream cool before sprinkling on the pistachios.

Serve cold.

Saffron Rice Pudding

Serves 6

* 125g (4½oz) short-grain round rice
* 1.5 litres (2½ pints) water
* 200g (7oz) sugar
* ¼ teaspoon saffron pistils or a good quality powdered saffron
* 1 tablespoon cornflour
* 3 tablespoons rose water (optional)
* 2 tablespoons raisins
* 2 tablespoons slivered or chopped pistachios
* 2 tablespoons slivered almonds

This is an almost jelly-like rice pudding with a wonderful delicate flavour, made with water, not milk. It is called zerde *in Turkey and* sholezard *in Iran.*

Boil the rice in the water for about 30 minutes, then add the sugar.

Mix the saffron with 1 tablespoon of boiling water and stir it in. Dissolve the cornflour in 3–4 tablespoons of cold water and pour into the pan, stirring vigorously. Continue to stir for a few minutes, until the liquid part thickens, then simmer on a low heat for 30 minutes. Add the rose water and stir in the raisins, pistachios and almonds.

Let it cool a little, then pour into a glass serving bowl.

Variation
* Add 1 teaspoon of cardamom seeds to the rice at the beginning.

Saffron Caramel Cream

Serves 6

* 600g (1 pint) milk
* 4oz sugar, plus 4 tablespoons
  more for the caramel
* a pinch of saffron pistils
* ¼ teaspoon cardamom seeds
* 2 tablespoons rose water
* 4 eggs, lightly beaten

A friend described the flavours of this cream which she tasted in an Iranian restaurant and I applied them to the classic crème caramel. It is magnificent.

Scald the milk with the sugar, saffron and cardamom and let it cool to lukewarm. Add the rose water and gradually beat into the eggs.

Heat the remaining 4 tablespoons of sugar in a small pan until it melts and becomes dark brown. Add 4 tablespoons of water. The liquid caramel will harden and then melt and bubble. Pour into a metal ring mould or other type of mould. Turn the mould around so that the caramel reaches every part, using a spoon to help spread it up the sides. Heating the mould in the oven beforehand keeps the caramel (which hardens as it cools) runny for longer.

Let the caramel cool before pouring in the milk mixture gently. Place the mould in a pan of water and bake in a 180°C (350°F, gas 4) oven for about 1 hour or until the custard has set. Chill before unmoulding.

To turn out, cut around the edges, place a serving dish on top, and turn upside down.

Pistachio Ice-cream

Serves 8–10

* 6 egg yolks
* 175g (7oz) sugar
* 600ml (1 pint) single cream
* 3 tablespoons rose water or to taste
* 150g (5oz) ground pistachios

This is not a traditional ice-cream but one developed here by compatriots from Egypt with traditional ingredients and flavourings. Some Indian and Middle Eastern stores sell blanched and slivered or ground pistachios. If they are not available you will have to blanch the pistachios for a few moments in boiling water to detach their skins, then peel them and grind them.

Beat the egg yolks and sugar to a thick pale cream. Bring the single cream to the boil in a pan and gradually pour over the yolk mixture, beating all the time. Pour the mixture back into the pan, place the pan inside another pan of boiling water, and stir until the mixture thickens into a custard.

Add the rose water and fold in the ground pistachios. Let the mixture cool, then pour it into a bowl lined with clingfilm. Cover with clingfilm and freeze overnight. Turn out 10–15 minutes before serving.

Note

* Some people cheat and use bought vanilla ice-cream. Blend it with the rose water and pistachios in the food processor, then freeze again.

Almond Ice-cream

Serves 8

* 150g (5oz) blanched almonds
* 300ml (10fl oz) milk
* 300ml (10fl oz) double cream
* 4 egg yolks
* 175g (6oz) sugar
* 2–3 tablespoons orange-blossom water
* 3 drops of almond essence

This too is a modern ice-cream.

Grind the almonds. Put them in a pan with the milk and cream and bring to the boil.

Beat the egg yolks with the sugar to a pale light cream, then pour in the milk mixture and continue to beat until well blended. Pour this back into the pan and stir constantly over a low heat until the mixture thickens to the consistency of custard – but do not let it boil or the yolks will curdle.

Add the orange-blossom water and the almond essence (pour the drops into a spoon first, as it is easy to pour too much and then the taste will be nasty). Let it cool. Pour into a bowl lined with clingfilm, cover with more clingfilm and freeze overnight. Turn out 10–15 minutes before serving.

Orange Ice-cream

Serves 6
* 8 egg yolks
* 125g (4¹⁄₂oz) sugar
* ¹⁄₂ litre (18fl oz) freshly squeezed orange juice

The base of this ice-cream is a custard made with egg yolks. Use freshly squeezed orange juice and make it the day before you want it.

Beat the egg yolks with the sugar to a pale thick cream.

Bring the orange juice to the boil in a pan, then pour it gradually over the egg yolk mixture, beating vigorously all the time. Pour back into the pan and stir constantly and vigorously over the lowest heat, without letting it boil, until the mixture thickens to a very light custard. Let it cool.

Line a mould with clingfilm and pour in the orange custard. Cover with clingfilm and put into the freezer.

Take the ice-cream out of the freezer 15 minutes before you are ready to serve and turn out on to a serving plate.

Sweet Couscous

Called mesfouf *in Tunisia and Algeria and* seffa *in Morocco, this is plain couscous, sometimes flavoured with honey or orange-blossom water, garnished with nuts and fresh or dried fruit. It is accompanied by hot milk to pour over. I eat it for breakfast.*

For 6–8 people prepare 500g (1lb 2oz) couscous as described on page 168, with the same volume of water (no salt). Stir in 3 tablespoons of butter and, if you like, 1 tablespoon of orange-blossom water.

Serve in a shallow bowl, shaped into a cone, accompanied by icing sugar and ground cinnamon to sprinkle on, a bowl of honey and a jug of hot milk. It is usual to present it sprinkled with icing sugar at the top and with lines of ground cinnamon coming down the sides.

Different garnishes to sprinkle on
* Plenty of fresh grapes.
* The pink seeds of 2 pomegranates.
* Semi-dried grapes or large table raisins or sultanas.
* About 150g (5oz) of blanched almonds, fried in oil until lightly golden, and coarsely chopped.
* 250g (8oz) dates.
* 300g (11oz) of mixed chopped nuts, including pistachios, walnuts and hazelnuts, and 75g (3oz) of raisins.

Konafa with Cheese

Serves 10 or more

* 500g (1lb) konafa (or kadaif)
  pastry
* 250g (8oz) unsalted butter,
  melted
* 100g (4oz) pistachio nuts,
  finely chopped, to garnish

For the syrup

* 500g (1lb) sugar
* 300ml (½ pint) water
* juice of ½ lemon
* 1 tablespoon orange-blossom
  water
* 1 tablespoon rose water

For the filling

* 500g (1lb) mozzarella cheese,
  grated or chopped
* 500g (1lb) unsalted ricotta
  cheese

Called kadaif *by Greeks and Turks, the dough for this pastry, which looks like soft white uncooked shredded wheat or vermicelli, can be bought in Middle Eastern stores. There are several traditional fillings. The one with a soft cheese makes a splendid hot dessert.*

To make the syrup, bring the sugar and water to the boil with the lemon juice and simmer for 10 minutes or until it is thick enough to coat a spoon. Add the orange-blossom and rose water and cook for 30 seconds more. Cool and chill in the refrigerator.

For the filling, mix the mozzarella and ricotta.

Put the konafa pastry in a large bowl. Pour the melted and slightly cooled butter over it and work it in very thoroughly with your fingers, pulling out and separating the strands and turning them over so that they do not stick together and are entirely coated with butter.

Spread half the pastry at the bottom of a 30cm (12in) round metal pan. Spread the cheese filling over it evenly and cover with the rest of the pastry, evening it out and flattening it with the palm of your hand so that it holds together compactly.

Bake in a preheated 180°C (350°F, gas 4) oven for 45 minutes, then turn up the oven to 230°C (450°F, gas 8) and bake for 15 minutes longer until the top is a light gold.

Remove from the oven and cut around the pastry with a sharp knife. Turn it out on to a large round serving plate and immediately pour the cold syrup all over the hot konafa. If you prefer, use only half the quantity – and let people add more syrup to their own portion themselves.

Serve hot or warm, sprinkled with the pistachio nuts.

Ghorayebah

Makes about 50

* 500g (1lb) unsalted butter
* 250g (8oz) caster sugar
* 625g (1¼lb) plain flour, sifted
* blanched almonds or pistachio nuts, to decorate

These delightful biscuity Arab pastries melt in the mouth. You must also try the version with ground hazelnuts.

Cream the butter and beat it until it becomes white. Add the sugar, beating constantly for about 5 minutes, until it is a smooth cream. Add the flour, gradually working it in by hand. Although no liquid is added, this makes a very soft dough. If the dough is too soft, add a little more flour.

Take walnut-sized lumps, roll them into balls and flatten them slightly. Place them on a baking tray, a little apart, as they spread slightly. Stick a blanched almond or pistachio on top of each one.

Bake in a 160°C (325°F, gas 3) oven for 20–30 minutes. Do not let the ghorayebah overcook. They must remain very white. They taste quite different if they are even slightly brown.

Variations

* A particularly delicious variation is to replace 120g (4oz) of the flour with 120g (4oz) of ground hazelnuts.
* You can flavour the dough with a grating of nutmeg or a teaspoon of ground cinnamon or ground cardamom.

Baklawa

Makes about 50 pieces

* 500g (1lb) filo pastry
* 180g (6oz) unsalted butter, melted
* 500g (1lb) pistachio nuts or walnuts, ground medium fine

For the syrup

* 500g (1lb) sugar
* 300ml (½ pint) water
* 2 tablespoons lemon juice
* 2 tablespoons orange-blossom or rose water

This is the all-time Middle Eastern pastry, but a home-made one is something other than the ubiquitous examples found in the trade.

Prepare the syrup first. Dissolve the sugar in the water with the lemon juice and simmer for a few minutes until it thickens enough to coat a spoon. Add orange-blossom or rose water and simmer for half a minute. Allow to cool, then chill in the refrigerator.

In a greased baking pan, a little smaller than the sheets of filo, lay half the sheets, one at a time, brushing each with melted butter and letting the edges come up the sides of the tray or overhang.

Spread the nuts of your choice evenly over the sheets. Cover with the remaining sheets, brushing each, including the top one, with melted butter. Cut parallel lines 4–5cm (1½in) apart diagonally into diamond shapes, using a sharp knife and cutting right through to the bottom.

Bake the baklawa in a preheated 180°C (350°F, gas 4) oven for 30–35 minutes or until it is puffed and lightly coloured. Remove from the oven and quickly pour the cold syrup over the hot baklawa along the slashed lines. The amount of syrup is the usual one. If you prefer to use less, pour on three-quarters or half the amount and let people help themselves to more if they wish.

When the baklawa is cold and ready to serve, cut along the lines again and lift the pieces of pastry out one by one on to a serving dish, or turn the whole pastry out first (by turning it upside down on to a large plate and then turning it over again on to the serving dish) and then cut again along the lines.

Variations

* *Kul-wa-shkur* ('eat and thank') is filled with ground blanched almonds mixed with half their weight in sugar. In this case use half the amount of syrup.
* In Iraq 1 or 2 teaspoons of ground cinnamon or ground cardamom are added to the chopped nuts.
* In Greece they stir a spoonful or two of honey into the syrup.

Almond 'Snake'

Serves 30 to 40

For the filling

* 1.5kg (3¹/₄lb) ground almonds
* 1kg (2lb 2oz) caster sugar
* 2 tablespoons ground cinnamon
* 200ml (7fl oz) orange-flower water
* a few drops of almond essence (optional)

For the pastry

* 500g (1lb) filo pastry
* 4¹/₂oz (125g) butter, melted
* 2 egg yolks for glazing

To garnish

* icing sugar
* 1 tablespoon ground cinnamon

This Moroccan pastry is a long coil – hence the name m'hencha, *meaning snake – of filo pastry filled with a ground almond paste. It is stunning to look at and exquisite. Make it for a grand occasion.*

Mix all the filling ingredients and work into a paste with your hands.

Open out the sheets of filo when you are ready to use them and keep them in a pile so that they do not dry out. Brush the top one lightly with melted butter. Take lumps of the almond paste and roll into fingers. Place them end to end in a line about 2cm (³/₄in) thick along one long edge and roll the sheet of filo up over the filling into a thin long roll, tucking the ends in to stop the filling oozing out.

Lift the roll up carefully with both hands and place it in the middle of a piece of greaseproof paper or greased sheet of foil on the largest possible oven sheet or tray. Curve the roll very gently like a snail – to do so without tearing the filo, you have to crease the pastry first like an accordion by pushing the ends of the rolls gently towards the centre with both hands.

Do the same with the other sheets until all the filling is used up, rolling them up with the filling inside, curving the rolls and placing them end to end to make a long tight coil.

Brush the top of the pastry with the egg yolks mixed with 2 teaspoons of water and bake in a 180°C (350°F, gas 4) oven for 35–40 minutes until crisp and lightly browned.

Serve cold, sprinkled with icing sugar and with lines of cinnamon in the shape of the spokes of a wheel.

Almond Fingers

Makes about 30

* 250g (8oz) ground almonds
* 120g (4oz) caster sugar, or to taste
* 3 tablespoons orange-blossom water
* 250g (8oz) filo pastry
* 90g (3oz) unsalted butter, melted
* icing sugar, to decorate

These exquisite Arab pastries are family favourites.

Mix the ground almonds with the sugar and orange-blossom water.

Cut the sheets of filo into 4 rectangular strips and pile them on top of each other so that they do not dry out. Brush the top one lightly with melted butter.

Put 1 heaped teaspoon of the almond mixture at one end of each rectangle. Roll up into a small cigar shape, folding the longer sides slightly over the filling midway. Place on a buttered baking tray and bake in a preheated 160°C (325°F, gas 3) oven for 30 minutes, or until lightly golden.

Serve cold, sprinkled with icing sugar.

Variation

* Other delicious fillings are chopped pistachios flavoured in the same way with sugar and orange-blossom water, and chopped walnuts mixed with sugar and a tablespoon of ground cinnamon.

Ma'amoul

Makes about 40

* 500g (1lb 2oz) plain flour
* 250g (9oz) unsalted butter
* 2–3 tablespoons orange-blossom water or rose water
* 4–5 tablespoons milk
* icing sugar, to sprinkle on

For the date filling

* 500g (1lb) pitted dates
* about 100ml (4fl oz) water

These glorious little stuffed pastries have a melt-in-the-mouth shell and a variety of fillings of dates or nuts – walnuts, pistachios or almonds. My mother always had a biscuit tin full of them to offer with coffee.

Prepare the filling. Cut the dates up into pieces. Put them into a saucepan with the water and cook over a low heat, stirring, until they turn to a soft paste. Let it cool.

Put the flour into a bowl and work in the butter with your fingers. Add the orange-blossom or rose water and the milk – just enough for the dough to hold together – and work until it is soft, malleable and easy to shape.

Take a walnut-sized lump of dough. Roll it into a ball and hollow it out with your thumb. Pinch the sides up to make a pot shape. Fill the hole with the filling to three-quarters full and bring the dough up over the opening to close into a ball. Flatten the filled balls slightly. Place the pastries on a large baking tray. Make little dents with the back of a fork. Bake in a preheated 160°C (325°F, gas 3) oven for 20–25 minutes. Do not let the pastries become brown or they will be hard and their taste will be spoilt. While they are still warm, they appear soft and uncooked, but on cooling they become firm.

When cold, dust with icing sugar. They will keep for a long time in a tightly closed tin.

Variations

These nut fillings are considered the grandest and they really are. Use them instead of the date filling.

* 375g (13oz) of finely chopped walnuts mixed with 4 tablespoons of sugar, 1 teaspoon of ground cinnamon and the grated rind of 1/2 an orange.

* 375g (13oz) of ground pistachio nuts mixed with 4 table-spoons of sugar and 1 tablespoon of rose water.
* 375g (13oz) of ground almonds mixed with 4 tablespoons of sugar and 2 tablespoons of rose or orange-blossom water.

Little Pistachio Cakes

Makes about 22

* 300g (10oz) shelled unsalted
  pistachios
* 200g (7oz) caster sugar
* 1–2 tablespoons orange-
  blossom water
* 2 whole eggs
* 2 egg yolks

These Tunisian pastries are deliciously soft and moist.

Grind the pistachios in the food processor. Add the rest of the
ingredients and blend well. Drop by the heaped tablespoon
into little paper cases and bake at 180°C (350°F, gas 4) for 25
minutes or until slightly firm.

Variation

* Use blanched almonds instead of pistachios and add 2–3
  drops of almond essence.

Dates Stuffed with Almond Paste

* 180g (6oz) ground almonds
* 90g (3oz) caster sugar
* 3–4 tablespoons rose or
  orange-blossom water
* 500g (1lb) dates

This is a sweetmeat to serve with coffee. Use a slightly moist variety of dried dates such as the Californian or Tunisian.

Mix the ground almonds and sugar in a bowl and add just enough rose or orange-blossom water to bind them into a firm paste. Put less than you seem to require, for once you start kneading with your hands the oil from the almonds will act as an extra bind. You can always add more as required.

Make a slit on one side of each date with a sharp knife and pull out the stone. Press in a small lump of almond paste and close the date slightly so as to reveal the filling.

Index